MacCain

Ley Tixtla 2018©Martin Rizzi
tragedyofmaccain@gmail.com

ISBN 978-1-61012-040-1

Design: Michael Godeck
Typeset in Ideal Sans
Title Font is Toxia

Front cover adapted from Ronald Gower's sculpture in Stratford-upon-Avon depicting Prince Hal.

Back cover adapted from Heath James 1834 engraving.

Back cover Chiện dich Phụng Hoàng "Phoenix Campaign" patch.

The Tragedy of
MacCain

by William Shakespeare

Chiringa Press
Seguin, Texas 2018

To my young friend and budding writer, Martin Rizzi

— *Separatio a mensa et a thalamo...*

Thucydides! bear thou witness to this classical tragedy; that it all proceeded from a singular incident of history: the cruel complicity of the Phoenix-network of the CIA in the assassination of President John Kennedy in Dallas. —MR

Act 1, Scene 1

A desert place

North Vietnam jungle clearing

Thunder and lightning. Enter three Witches.

First Witch

When shall we three meet again
In thunder, lightning, or in rain?

Second Witch

When the hurlyburly's done,
When the battle's lost and won.

Third Witch

That will be ere the set of sun.

First Witch

Where the place?

Second Witch

In the black rain.

Third Witch

There to meet with MacCain.

First Witch

I come, Graymalkin!

Second Witch

Paddock calls.

Third Witch

Anon.

All

Fair is foul, and foul is fair:
Hover through the fog and filthy air.

Exeunt

Act 1 Scene 2

Washington D.C. White House.
President John Kennedy, Walt Rostow

John Kennedy

Whence camest thou, worthy sir?

Allen Dulles

From Nam, great President;
Where the Communist banners flout the sky
And fan our people cold. Giap himself,
With terrible numbers,
Assisted by that most disloyal traitor
The Viet Cong, began a dismal conflict;
Till our clandestine assassination operations
Confronted the Viet upstart with self-comparisons
Point against point rebellious, arm 'gainst arm.
Curbing his lavish spirit: and, to conclude,
The victory fell on us.

John Kennedy

Great happiness!

Allen Dulles

Ho asked for a reprieve from our bombing
But as we had already reported the body count
We would not deign him access to a hot line
Till he disbursed into a BCCI account
Ten millions of dollars to our general use.

9

John Kennedy

You are altogether too mercantile professor!
Yet, congratulations on this military victory.

Allen Dulles

Special operations is the hawk of war today
Operation Phoenix worked as was pretended.

John Kennedy

Your special operations forces merit astonishment.
What the Commies lost, was gained by MacCain.

Exeunt

Act 1 Scene 2 — Part 2

Vietnam jungle clearing.

Enter Special Operations Commandos.

Thomas Clines

Operation Phoenix unit. Identify yourself!

Two insect bitten prisoners in tiger cages.
Their pales skeletons stares are horrifying.

Felix Rodríguez

What a haste looks through his eyes!
That seems to speak things strange.

Apodeka stares back, his tortured body is totally covered with
sores. He can't stretch his body out, as he is cages in an impos-
sibly cramped position.

Victor Apodeca

Air Lieutenant Victor Apodeca sir.

Oliver North

Ours is an elite mission, Air Lieutenant,
Where is air man MacCain?

Felix Rodríguez

Is he in a torture chamber?
The Commies will pay for his mistreatment.

Thomas Clines

Well, speak. Is MacCain under torture?
His dad will not like to hear that.

Victor Apodeca

He was in it. For a minute. And he was out.
Now they sound that damned announcement:
His recorded messages of reconciliation with our captors,
Day and night at this hateful camp.

Felix Rodríguez

Well, where is he? You know his is royal blood.

Victor Apodeca

In that compound over there.

Felix Rodríguez

He is? Stay where you are then.

Exeunt soldiers and their commanders.

Act 1 Scene 2 — Part 3

A young and fit looking John MacCain dips a fried chicken wing into a dish of pungent red sauce. He smacks his lips just as he turns toward a slender young Vietnamese woman with one of her breasts exposed.

Just then, a flash-bang grenade, thrown by the Special Forces commandos, explodes in the room! The bamboo door comes crashing in to the sound of martial shouts. Heard are the loud barks of an officer, as strong men manhandle MacCain, hustling him out the door, and into the darkness of jungle night.

Exeunt all except the Vietnamese girl.

Act 1 Scene 3

A jungle in Vietnam.

Thunder. Enter the three Witches

First Witch

Where hast thou been, sister?

Second Witch

Killing swine.

Third Witch

Sister, where thou?

First Witch

A sailor's wife had chestnuts in her lap,
And munch'd, and munch'd, and munch'd:—
'*Give me,*' quoth I:
'*Aroint thee, witch!*' the rump-fed ronyon cries.
Her husband's to Aleppo gone, master o' the Tiger:
But in a sieve I'll thither sail,
And, like a rat without a tail,
I'll do, I'll do, and I'll do.

Second Witch

I'll give thee a wind.

First Witch

Thou'rt kind.

Third Witch

And I another.

First Witch

Blow me by way of Iskaroon
I will look in at the safe house
There of the takfiri mercenaries
Nine times nine, dwindle, peak and pine:
Though his canoe cannot be lost,
Yet it shall be tempest-tost.
Look what I have.

Second Witch

Show me, show me.

First Witch

Here I have a pilot's thumb,
Wreck'd the Ship of State as homeward he did come.
It begins to rain...

Third Witch

The rain! the rain!
here comes MacCain!

All

The weird sisters, hand in hand,
Posters of the sea and land,
Thus do go about, about:
Thrice to thine and thrice to mine
And thrice again, to make up nine
It is explained at the secret society.
Peace! the charm's wound up.

   Enter MacCain and Colby...

MacCain

So foul and fair a day I have not seen.

Colby Consults GPS.

This is the pick-up zone? And what are these
So wither'd and so wild in their attire,
with white brows clenched in confident thought?
They look not like the Viets I've seen.
Are you real? or are you something
A man may question? You seem to understand me,
By each at once her chappy finger laying
Upon her skinny lips: you should be women,
And yet your beards forbid me to interpret
That you are so.

MacCain

Speak, if you can: what are you?

First Witch

All hail, MacCain! hail to thee, Full Admiral in the Navy!

Second Witch

All hail, MacCain, hail to thee, Senator from Arizona!

Third Witch

All hail, MacCain, thou shalt be President of the United States!

Colby

Good sir, why do you start; and seem to fear
Things that do sound so fair? I' the name of truth,
Are you a holographic apparition of the Soviets?
From some Russian spoon-bending laboratory?

My noble partner here you greet with present grace and great
Prediction of the achievement of great ambition,
To such an effect that he seems rapt.
To me you speak not.

Act 1, Scene 3

If you can look into the seeds of time,
And say which grain will grow and which will not,
Speak then to me, who neither beg nor fear
Your favours nor your hate.

Still, I am curious.

First Witch

Hello!

Second Witch

Hello!

Third Witch

Hello!

First Witch

Lesser than MacCain, and greater.

Second Witch

Not so happy, yet much happier.

Third Witch

You will make kings, not be one yourself.
So all hail, MacCain and Colby!

Witches

All hail!

MacCain

Stay, you imperfect speakers, tell me more:
By golly I know I am in line for an Admiralty;
But Senator of Arizona? That's Barry Goldwater
A very well established gentleman; and to be Senator
Stands not within the prospect of belief,
No more than to be President.

Say from whence you owe this strange intelligence?
Or why upon this jungle clearing you stop our way
With such prophetic greeting? Speak, I charge you.

Witches vanish...

Colby

The earth hath bubbles, as the water has,
And these are of them. Whither are they vanish'd?

MacCain

Into the air; and what seem'd corporal melted
As breath into the wind. Would they had stay'd!

Colby

Were such things here as we do speak about?
Or have we eaten on the insane root
That takes the reason prisoner?

MacCain

I could use some.

Colby

You shall be Senator.

MacCain

And President too: went it not so?

Colby

To the selfsame tune and words. Who's here?

Enter John McCone and Walt Rostow...

John McCone

The President hath happily received, MacCain,

The news of thy success; and when he reads
of your personal adventure in the anti-insurgent fight
His wonders and his praises do contend
Which should be thine or his: silenced with that,
In viewing o'er the rest o' the selfsame day,
He finds thee saved from the prison camp
Nothing afeard of what thyself didst make,
Strange images of death. As thick as hail
Came post with post; and every one did bear
Thy praises in his country's great defence,
And from diplomatic pouches
Poured them down before him.

Walt Rostow

To give thee from the Commander in Chief, thanks;
Only to herald thee into his sight,
Not pay thee.
And, for an earnest of a greater honour,
He bade me, from him, to tell you that you are in line to be a
Full Admiral in the Navy. For it is thine.

Colby

What, can the devil speak true?

MacCain

There are many senior candidates for Admiral:
Why do you dress me in borrow'd robes?

Walt Rostow

Yes but some are under heavy judgment for not supporting the
increase in rhythm of this war,
Those timid souls deserve to lose preference in appointment.
Some are keeping their heads out of the line of fire giving aid
to the enemy and sympathizing with them.
Only a Congressional hearing could ascertain to what extent
they have labour'd in his country's wreck, I know not;

But treasons capital, confess'd and proved,
Have overthrown many enemies who clad themselves
in the thin cloak of idealism...

MacCain *[Aside]*

Senator and President!

  To Walt Rostow and John McCone

Thanks for your pains.

[To Colby] Do you not hope you will be the maker of kings
When those that gave the Presidency to me
Promised no less to you?

Colby

But 'tis strange:
And oftentimes, to win us to our harm,
The instruments of darkness tell us truths,
Win us with honest trifles, to betray's
In deepest consequence.
Cousins, a word, I pray you.

MacCain *[Aside]*

Two truths are told,
As happy prologues to the swelling act
Of the imperial theme. —I thank you, gentlemen.
Cannot be ill, cannot be good: if ill,
Why hath it given me earnest of success,
Commencing in a truth? I am to be an Admiral:
If good, why do I yield to that suggestion
Whose horrid image doth unfix my hair
And make my seated heart knock at my ribs,
Against the use of nature? Present fears
Are less than horrible imaginings:
My thought, whose murder yet is but fantastical,
Shakes so my single state of man that function

Is smother'd in surmise, and nothing is
But what is not.

Colby

Look, how our partner's rapt.

MacCain *[Aside]*

If chance will have me Senator, why, chance may crown me,
Without my doing anything.

Colby

He is breathing the air of destiny; just like
our clothes only fit when we have worn them.

MacCain *[Aside]*

Come what come may,
Time and the hour runs through the roughest day.

Barry Seal

Worthy MacCain, the copter is ready to take off.

MacCain

Give me your favour: my dull brain was wrought
With things forgotten.
Kind gentlemen, your pains
Are register'd where every day I turn
The leaf to read them.
Let us toward the President
Think upon what hath chanced, and, at another time,
The interim having weigh'd it, let us speak
Our free hearts each to other.

Colby

Very gladly.

MacCain

Till then, enough. Come, friends.

Exeunt

Act 1 Scene 4

Washington DC White House

Flourish. Enter President John Kennedy, Bobby Kennedy, Robert McNamara, Walt Rostow, Allen Dulles, and Staffers.

President John Kennedy

Has the mission to Saigon reported? Are not
Those in commission yet return'd to Washington?

Robert McNamara

My liege,
They are not yet come back. But I have spoke
With one that saw filed reports where the Viet Cong
Admit how badly they were hurt in their offensives.
They are sorry they ever set on this reckless course
This unnecessary defiance of the United States
And everything that it stands for. A deep repentance
Must be that of that loser Diem and his no good brother;
Nothing in his life will become them like
The leaving of it; he died! Imagine
To throw away the dearest thing he owed,
As 'twere a careless trifle.

President John Kennedy

There's no art
To find the mind's construction in the face:
He was a gentleman on whom I built
An absolute trust.

Enter MacCain, Colby, Peter Desalvo, and Gen. Lansdale...

Act 1, Scene 4

Come in gentlemen!
I owe you all a lot for successfully settling these matters.
I wish the Diem brothers had not been killed however I
understand as you have explained it to me that this was an
unavoidable circumstances.
You may well think that your recompense is slow to overtake
thee. Indeed, I wish you deserved less.
So I don't have to give you so many thanks and I don't have to
negotiate a hefty recompense you did almost too much!
All I have left to say is that more is thy due than more than all
can pay.

MacCain

The service and the loyalty I owe,
In doing it, pays itself. Your honor's part
Is to receive our duties; and our duties
Are to your throne and state children and servants,
Which do but what they should, by doing every thing
Safe toward your love and honour.

John Kennedy

Welcome hither:
I have begun to plant thee, and will labour
To make thee full of growing. Noble Colby,
That hast no less deserved, nor must be known
No less to have done so, let me enfold thee
And hold thee to my heart.

Colby

There if I grow,
The harvest is your own.

John Kennedy

Have the prisoners of war then been released?

MacCain

Yes. We are in negotiation with their captors.

John Kennedy

I enjoin them to you; brave men
Who were called to arms in a strange land.

MacCain

We will never abandon Americans
Who have been captured by Communists.

John Kennedy

My plentious joys,
Wanton in fullness, seek to hide themselves
In drops of sorrow. Staffers, supporters, the gentlemen and the
ladies of Washington
And you whose places are the nearest, know
We will establish our estate upon
Our eldest, brother Robert, whom we name hereafter
Attorney General to enforce my planned continuation of the
Legacy of Franklin D Roosevelt's New Deal
And the General Welfare Clause in the Preamble
To the United States Constitution which honour must not
Unaccompanied invest him only,
But signs of nobleness, like stars, shall shine
On all deservers. From hence to your Penthouse
For a Press Availability and bind us further to you.
Would that it were other, however, our schedule will not let us
Stay here more than a single night.

MacCain

Well now it is to work the plan
I'll be myself the harbinger
and make joyful The hearing of my wife
with your approach; So humbly take my leave.

John Kennedy

My worthy sir!

MacCain

[Aside] Bobby Kennedy, the heir apparent! that is a step on
which I must fall down, or else o'erleap,
For in my way it lies. Stars, hide your fires;
Let not light see my black and deep desires:
The eye wink at the hand; yet let that be,
Which the eye fears, when it is done, to see.

Exit MacCain

John Kennedy

True, worthy Colby; he is full, so valiant,
And in his commendations I am fed;
It is a banquet to me. Let's after him,
Whose care is gone before to bid us welcome:
he's a redoubtable bones man with great coke;
there are betimes some crazy ladies at his place.

Flourish
Exeunt

Act 1 Scene 5
MacCain's Luxury Apartment in New York

Enter George HW Bush

George HW Bush

They met me in the day of success: and I have
learned by the perfectest report, they have more in
them than mortal knowledge. When I burned in desire
to question them further, they made themselves air,
into which they vanished. While I stood rapt in
the wonder of it, came missives from the king, who
all-hailed me *'Admiral of the Navy;'* by which title,
before, these weird sisters saluted me, and referred
me to the coming on of time, with *'Hail, President that
shalt be!'* This have I thought good to deliver
thee, my dearest partner of greatness, that thou
mightst not lose the dues of rejoicing, by being
ignorant of what greatness is promised thee.
Lay it to thy heart, and farewell.
Admiral thou art, Senator and President shalt be
What thou art promised: yet do I fear thy nature;
It is too full o' the milk of human kindness
To catch the nearest way: thou wouldst be great;
You are not without ambition, but without
The illness should attend it: what thou wouldst highly,
That wouldst thou holily; wouldst not play false,
And yet wouldst wrongly win: thou'ldst have, great Admiral,
That which cries *'Thus thou must do, if thou have it; And that
which rather thou dost fear to do*

Than wishest should be undone.' Hie thee hither,
That I may pour my spirits in thine ear;
And chastise with the valor of my tongue
All that impedes thee from the golden round,
Which fate and metaphysical aid doth seem
To have thee crown'd withal.

Enter a Messenger

What is your tidings?

Messenger

The President comes here to-night.

George HW Bush

Thou'rt mad to say it:
Is not thy master with him? who, were't so,
Would have inform'd for preparation.

Messenger

So please you, it is true: our thane is coming:
One of my fellows had the speed of him,
Who, almost dead for breath, had scarcely more
Than would make up his message.

George HW Bush

Give him tending;
He brings great news.

Exit Messenger...

George HW Bush

The raven himself is hoarse
That croaks the fatal entrance of Kennedy
Under my battlements. Come, you spirits
That tend on mortal thoughts, unsex me here,

And fill me from the crown to the toe top-full
Of direst cruelty! Make thick my blood;
Stop up the access and passage to remorse,
That no compunctious visitings of nature
Shake my fell purpose, nor keep peace between
The effect and it! Come to my woman's breasts,
And take my milk for gall, you murdering ministers,
Wherever in your sightless substances
You wait on nature's mischief! Come, thick night,
And pall thee in the dunnest smoke of hell,
That my keen knife see not the wound it makes,
Nor heaven peep through the blanket of the dark,
To cry 'Hold, hold!'

Enter MacCain...

Great Admiral! worthy Senator!
Greater than both, by the all-hail hereafter!
Thy letters have transported me beyond
This ignorant present, and I feel now
The future in the instant.

MacCain

My dearest love,
Kennedy comes here to-night.

George HW Bush

And when goes hence?

MacCain

To-morrow, as he purposes.

George HW Bush

O, never shall sun that morrow see!
Your face, my thane, is as a book where men
May read strange matters. To beguile the time,

Act 1, Scene 5

Look like the time; bear welcome in your eye,
Your hand, your tongue: look like the innocent flower,
But be the serpent under't.
He that's coming Must be provided for: and you shall put
This night's great business into my dispatch;
Which shall to all our nights and days to come
Give solely sovereign sway and masterdom.

MacCain

We will speak further.

George HW Bush

Only look up clear; To alter favour ever is to fear:
Leave all the rest to me.

Exeunt

Act 1 Scene 6

Before MacCain's Luxury Apartments

Hautboys and torches. Enter John Kennedy, Colby, Bobby Kennedy, Walt Rostow, Robert McNamara, Allen Dulles, John McCone, and Security.

John Kennedy

This Penthouse hath a pleasant seat; the air
Nimbly and sweetly recommends itself
Unto our gentle senses.

Colby

This guest of summer,
The temple-haunting martlet, does approve,
By his loved mansionry, that the heaven's breath
Smells wooingly here: no jutty, frieze,
Buttress, nor coign of vantage, but this bird
Hath made his pendent bed and procreant cradle:
Where they most breed and haunt, I have observed.
The air is delicate.

Enter Lady MacCain...

John Kennedy

See, see, our honour'd hostess!
The love that follows us sometime is our trouble,
Which still we thank as love. Herein I teach you
How you shall bid God 'ild us for your pains,
And thank us for your trouble.

Act 1, Scene 6

Lady MacCain

All our service
In every point twice done and then done double
Were poor and single business to contend
Against those honours deep and broad wherewith
Your majesty loads our house: for those of old,
And the late dignities heap'd up to them,
We rest your hermits.

John Kennedy

Where's the Admiral?
We were on his heels, and had a purpose
To be his purveyor: but his private jet is too fast;
And his great love, sharp as his spur, hath help't him to his
home before us. Fair and noble hostess,
We are your guest to-night.

Lady MacCain

Your servants ever have theirs,
themselves and what is theirs, in compt, to
make their audit at your pleasure Mr. President,
Still to return your own.

John Kennedy

Give me your hand;
Conduct me to mine host: we love him highly,
And shall continue our graces towards him.
By your leave, hostess.

Exeunt

Act 1 Scene 7

MacCain's Luxury Apartment in New York

Hautboys and torches. Marilyn Monroe and Judith Baker. Enter a Server, and divers Servants with dishes and service, and pass over the stage. Then enter MacCain.

MacCain

If it were done when 'tis done, then 'twere well
It were done quickly: if the assassination
Could trammel up the consequence, and catch
With his surcease success; that but this blow
Might be the be-all and the end-all here,
But here, upon this bank and shoal of time,
We'd jump the life to come. But in these cases
We still have judgment here; that we but teach
Bloody instructions, which, being taught, return
To plague the inventor: this even-handed justice
Commends the ingredients of our poison'd chalice
To our own lips as an American who would never
be disloyal to our beloved fiefdom
as the fine babes and crank are only recreational.
Besides, this Kennedy hath borne his faculties so meek,
hath been so clear in his great office,
that his virtues will plead like angels, trumpet-tongued,
Against the deep damnation of his taking-off;
and pity, like a naked new-born babe,

Striding the blasting winds in the air
choruses of a cappella singers from heaven

fourwheeling on sightless couriers of political storm
that shall blow the horrid deed in every eye,
That tears shall drown the wind. Yet I cant resist
seizing the main chance on account of
Vaulting ambition, which o'erleaps itself
And falls on the other.

Enter George HW Bush...

How now! What news?

George HW Bush

He has almost supp'd:
why have you left the chamber?

MacCain

Hath he ask'd for me?

George HW Bush

You know he has.

MacCain

We will proceed no further in this business:
He hath honour'd me of late; and I have bought
Golden opinions from all sorts of people,
Which would be worn now in their newest gloss,
Not cast aside so soon. My career is going up dear.

George HW Bush

Was the hope drunk
Wherein you dress'd yourself? Hath it slept since?
And wakes it now, to look so green and pale
At what it did so freely? From this time
Such I account thy love when you want to snug with me.
Art thou afeard to be the same in thine own act and valor
As thou art in desire?
Wouldst thou have your imperial destiny

Or live a coward in thine own esteem?

MacCain

Prithee, peace:
I dare do all that may become a man;
Who dares do more is none.

George HW Bush

What beast was't, then,
That made you break this enterprise to me?
When you durst do it, then you were a man;
And, to be more than what you were, you would
Be so much more the man. Nor time nor place
Did then adhere, and yet you would make both:
They have made themselves, and that their fitness now does
unmake you.
I have given suck, and know how tender 'tis to love the babe
that milks me: I would, while it was smiling in my face,
Have pluck'd my nipple from his boneless gums,
And dash'd the brains out, had I so sworn as you
Have done to this.

MacCain

If we should fail?

George HW Bush

We fail!
But screw your courage to the sticking-place,
And we'll not fail. When Kennedy is asleep—
Whereto the rather shall his tempress
warmly invite him to visit Cabell's Dallas
—where at midnight he awaits that stripper
wanting to unpackage where there's no public.
He knows the stuff I give him is the best
and his brain shall be a fume, and reason
A pinprick only: when semi-consciousness

Their drenched natures allow their own death.
What cannot you and I perform upon
The unguarded Kennedy? What not put upon
His spongy officers, who shall bear the guilt
Of our great event?

MacCain

Bring forth men-children only;
For thy undaunted mettle should compose
Nothing but males. Will it not be received,
When we have mark'd with blood that sleepy cop Oswald who
has been tailing our counter revolutionaries and when the
patrolman Tippet is kil'd in cold blood.
That they have done't?

George HW Bush

Who dares receive it other,
As we shall make our griefs and clamour roar
Upon his death

MacCain

I am settled, and alerted the Corsican shooters
And the backup unit to get ready for this terrible feat.
Away, and mock the time with fairest show:
False face must hide what the false heart doth know.

Exeunt

Act 2, Scene 1

Lobby of MacCain's Luxury High Rise Apartment

Enter Colby, and Shackley aiming a tiny flashlight before him…

Colby
How goes the night, boy?

Shackley
The moon is down; I have not heard the clock.

Colby
And she goes down at twelve.

Shackley
I take't, 'tis later, sir.

Colby
Hold, take my shooter. There's husbandry in heaven;
Their lights are all out. Take thee that too.
A heavy summons lies like lead upon me,
And yet I would not sleep: merciful powers,
Restrain in me the cursed thoughts that nature
Gives way to in repose!

Enter MacCain and a Servant with a torch…

Give me my gun.
Who's there?

MacCain
A friend.

Colby

What, John not yet at rest? Kennedy's a-bed:
He hath been in unusual pleasure, and
Sent forth great largess to your offices.
He greets your wife withal,
By the name of most kind hostess;
And shut up in measureless content
With two tall blondes.

MacCain

I was almost flat footed, he walked right into it
If he had not walked in himself, I might doubt
That he had not cast himself adrift upon eternity.

Colby

All's well.
I dreamt last night of the three weird sisters:
To you they have show'd some truth.

MacCain

I think not of them:
Yet, when we have an hour
over some johnny walker blacks,
We would spend that time
 in some words upon that business.

Colby

At your kind'st leisure.

MacCain

If you take my orders when the time comes
It shall make honour for you with the skull and bones crew.

Colby

Its all good.
I still keep my bosom franchised and allegiance clear,
I shall be counsell'd.

MacCain
Relax meanwhile.

Colby
Thanks, sir: the like to you!

Exit Colby and Shackley...

MacCain

He presses a button and while holding the button down. He speaks into a small box...

Go bid thy mistress, when my drink is ready,
She strike upon the bell. Get thee to bed.

Is this a high powered rifle which I see before me,
The gunstock toward my hand?
Come, let me clutch thee.
I have thee not, and yet I see thee still.
Art thou not, fatal vision, sensible
To feeling as to sight? or art thou but
A weapon of the mind, a false creation,
Proceeding from the heat-oppressed brain?
I see thee yet, in form as palpable
As this which now I draw.
Thou marshall'st me the way that I was going;
And such an instrument I was to use.
Mine eyes are made the fools o' the other senses,
Or else worth all the rest; I see thee still,
And on thy crosshairs gouts of blood,
Which was not so before. There's no such thing:
It is the bloody business which informs
Thus to mine eyes. Now o'er the one halfworld
Nature seems dead, and wicked dreams abuse
The curtain'd sleep; satanism of process church

and wither'd murder, Alarum'd by his sentinel, the wolf, Whose
howl's his watch, thus with his stealthy pace. With ravishing
strides, towards his design, Henry Lucas moved like a ghost.
Thou sure and firm-set earth,
Hear not my steps, which way they walk,
for fear thy very stones prate of my whereabout,
And take the present horror from the time,
Which now suits with it. Whiles I threat, he lives:
Words to the heat of deeds too cold a breath gives.

A bell rings...

I go, and it is done; the bell invites me.
Hear it not, Kennedy; for it is a knell
That summons thee to heaven or to hell.

Exeunt

Act 2 Scene 2

The same.

Enter Lady MacCain.

Lady MacCain

That which hath made them drunk hath made me bold;
What hath quench'd them hath given me fire. Hark! Peace!
It was the owl that shriek'd, the fatal bellman,
Which gives the stern'st good-night. He is about it:
The doors are open; and the surfeited grooms
Do mock their charge with snores: I have drugg'd
their possets,
That death and nature do contend about them,
Whether they live or die.

MacCain

[Within] Who's there? What, ho!

Lady MacCain

Alack, I am afraid they have awaked,
And 'tis not done. The attempt and not the deed confounds
us. Hark! I laid their weapons ready;
They could not miss with them. Asleep in my hands!
I could off him myself and have the personal pleasure .

Enter MacCain...

What?

MacCain

The deed is done.

Didst thou not hear a noise?

Lady MacCain

I heard the owl scream and the crickets cry.
Did not you speak?

MacCain

When?

Lady MacCain

Now.

MacCain

As I descended?

Lady MacCain

Ay.

MacCain

Hark!
Who lies i' the second chamber?

Lady MacCain

Bobby

MacCain

This is a sorry sight.

> *Looking on his hands...*

Lady MacCain

A foolish thought, to say a sorry sight.

MacCain

At the Carousel Club one of the secret service detail nodded
off, did laugh in's sleep,

and his partner who had passed out cried *'Murder!'*
That they did wake each other:
I stood and heard them:
But they did say their prayers,
and address'd them again to sleep.

Lady MacCain

Those two stay together at the Holiday Inn...

MacCain

One cried *'God Bless America!'*
and *'Right On'* the other;
In the morning they have to see
how they had been set up
Listening their fear, I could not say *'Secure'*
When they did say *'All secure?'*

Lady MacCain

Consider it not so deeply.

MacCain

But wherefore could not I pronounce *'Secure'*?
I had most need of cover, and *'Secure'*
Stuck in my throat.

Lady MacCain

These deeds must not be thought
After these ways; so, it will make us mad.

MacCain

Methought I heard a voice cry *'Sleep no more!*
MacCain does murder sleep', the innocent sleep,
Sleep that knits up the ravell'd sleeve of care,
The death of each day's life, sore labour's bath,
Balm of hurt minds, great nature's second course,
Chief nourisher in life's feast —

Lady MacCain

What do you mean?

MacCain

Still it cried *'Sleep no more!'* to all the house:
*'MacCain hath murder'd sleep, and therefore
shall sleep no more; MacCain shall sleep no more.'*

Lady MacCain

Who was it that thus cried? Why, worthy sir
You do unbend your noble strength, to think
So brainsickly of things. Go get some water,
And wash this filthy witness from your hand.
Why did you bring these rapekits from the place?
They must lie there: go carry them; and smear
The sleeping secret servicemen with this blood.

MacCain

I'll go no more:
I am afraid to think what I have done;
Look on't again I dare not.

Lady MacCain

Infirm of purpose!
Give me the rapekits: the sleeping and the dead
Are but as pictures: 'tis the eye of childhood
That fears a painted devil. If he do bleed,
I'll gild the faces of the guards withal;
this will eliminate them as witnesses.

> *Exit Lady MacCain. The sound of a buzzer.
> Again the sound. Again. Again, insistently...*

MacCain

Whence is that buzzing?

How is't with me, when every noise appalls me?
What hands are here? Ha! They pluck out mine eyes.
Will all great Neptune's ocean wash this blood
Clean from my hand? No, this my hand will rather
make a red stain that spreads throughout the water.

   Re-enter Lady MacCain...

Lady MacCain

My hands are of your colour; but I shame
To wear a heart so white.

   The buzzing continues...

I hear a buzzing
At the south entry: retire we to our chamber;
A little water clears us of this deed:
How easy is it, then!
Leave it to the Warren Commission.

   Buzzing, buzzing...

Hark! more buzzing.
Get on your nightgown, lest occasion call us,
And show us to be watchers. Be not lost
So poorly in your thoughts.

MacCain

To know my deed, 'twere best not know myself.
Wake JFK with thy buzzing! I would thou couldst!

   Exeunt

Act 2 Scene 3

The same.

Buzzing is Heard ... Enter a Doorman.

Doorman

Here's a buzzing indeed!
If a man were porter of hell-gate,
he should get old turning the key.

Buzzing continues...

Buzz, buzz, buzz! Who's there, i' the name of
Beelzebub? Here's a farmer, that hanged
Himself on the expectation of plenty
When the credit default swaps he bought went South.
Come in time; bring your overcoat; here you'll sweat for't.

Buzzing continues...

Buzz, Buzz! Who's there, in the other devil's
name? Faith, here's an equivocator, that could
swear in both the scales against either scale;
who committed treason enough for God's sake,
yet could not equivocate to heaven: O, come
in, equivocator.

Buzzing continues...

Buzz, buzz, buzz! Who's there? Faith, here's an
English tailor come hither, for stealing out of
a French house: come in, tailor; here you may
roast your goose.

Buzzing continues

Buzz, buzz; never at quiet! What are you? But this place is too cold for hell. I'll devil-porter it no further: I had thought to have let in some of all professions that go the primrose way to the everlasting bonfire.

    Buzzing continues...

Anon, anon! I pray you,
remember the doorman.

    Opens the door
    Enter Bobby Kennedy and Martin Luther King...

Bobby Kennedy

Was it so late, friend, ere you went to bed,
That you do lie so late?

Doorman

'Faith sir, we were carousing till the
second cock: and drink, sir, is a great
provoker of three things.

Bobby Kennedy

What three things does drink especially provoke?

Doorman

Marry, sir, nose-painting, sleep, and urine.
Lechery, sir, it provokes, and unprovokes;
It provokes the desire, but it takes away
The performance: therefore, much drink
May be said to be an equivocator with lechery:
It makes him, and it mars him;
It sets him on, and it takes him off; it persuades him, and
Disheartens him; makes him stand to, and not stand to;
In conclusion, equivocates him
In a sleep, and, giving him the lie, leaves him.

Bobby Kennedy

I believe drink gave thee the lie last night.

Doorman

That it did, sir, i' the very throat on me:
But I go give him back his lie; and, I think,
It was too strong for him,
Though he took up my legs sometime,
Yet I made a shift to cast him.

Bobby Kennedy

Is your Boss stirring?

Enter MacCain...

Our buzzing has awaked him; here he comes.

Martin Luther King

Good morrow, noble sir.

MacCain

Good morrow, both.

Bobby Kennedy

Is the President stirring, worthy sir?

MacCain

Not yet.

Bobby Kennedy

He did command me to call timely on him:
I have almost slipp'd the hour.

MacCain

I'll bring you to him.

Act 2, Scene 3

Bobby Kennedy
I know this is a joyful trouble to you;
But yet 'tis one.

MacCain
The labour we delight in physics pain.
Here is the private elevator to his apartments.

Bobby Kennedy
I'll make so bold to call,
For 'tis my limited service.

Exit Bobby Kennedy...

Martin Luther King
Goes the President hence to-day?

MacCain
He does: he did appoint so.

Martin Luther King
The night has been unruly: where we lay,
Our chimneys were blown down; and, as they say,
Lamentings heard i' the air; strange screams of death,
And prophesying with accents terrible
Of dire combustion and confused events
New hatch'd to the woeful time: the obscure bird
Clamour'd the livelong night: some say, the earth
Was feverous and did shake.

MacCain
'Twas a rough night.

Martin Luther King
My young remembrance cannot parallel
A fellow to it.

Re-enter Bobby Kennedy...

Bobby Kennedy

O horror, horror, horror! Tongue nor heart
Cannot conceive nor name thee!

MacCain

What's the matter?

Bobby Kennedy

Confusion now hath made his masterpiece!
Most sacrilegious murder hath broke open
The nation's anointed temple, and stole thence
The life o' the building!

MacCain

What is 't you say? the life?

Martin Luther King

Mean you the President?

Bobby Kennedy

Approach the chamber, and destroy your sight.
Do not bid me speak;
See, and then speak yourselves.

Exit MacCain and Martin Luther King...

Awake, awake!
Ring the alarum-bell. Murder and treason!
Colby and Shackley! Kissinger! Awake!
Shake off this downy sleep, death's counterfeit,
And look on death itself! Up, up, and see the
Texas School Book Depostory! Kissinger! Colby!
As from your graves rise up
To take a look at this horror! Ring the bell.

Act 2, Scene 3

Bell rings...
Enter Lady MacCain...

Lady MacCain

What's the business,
That such a hideous trumpet calls to parley
The sleepers of the house? Speak, speak!

Bobby Kennedy

O gentle lady,
Tis not for you to hear what I can speak:
The repetition, in a woman's ear,
Would murder as it fell.

Enter Colby...

O Colby, Colby,
The President's murder'd!

Lady MacCain

Woe, alas! What, in our house?

Colby

Too cruel anywhere.
Dear Bobby, I prithee, contradict thyself,
And say it is not so.

Re-enter MacCain and Martin Luther King, with Theodore
Shackley...

MacCain

Had I but died an hour before this chance,
I had lived a blessed time; for, from this instant,
There 's nothing serious in mortality:
All is but toys; renown and grace is dead!
The wine of life is drawn, and the yucky stuff
At the bottom is all that is left in this vault to brag of.

Enter Bobby Kennedy and Ted Kennedy...

Ted Kennedy

What is amiss?

MacCain

You are, and do not know't:
The spring, the head, the fountain of your blood
Is stopp'd; the very source of it is stopp'd.

Bobby Kennedy

The President is murder'd.

Ted Kennedy

O, by whom?

Shackley

A lone nut. A disgruntled person was picked up escaping the
scene in his fevered flight from the assassination he shot a cop
and ran into to the Texas Theater. The people only stared,
and were distracted; a snake in the grass Fair Play For Cuba
Communist agent, ever to be feared, never trusted.

MacCain

O, yet I do repent me of that fury,
That the killer was further murdered

Bobby Kennedy

How did it happen?

MacCain

Who can be wise, amazed, temperate and furious,
Loyal and neutral, in a moment? no man.
The violent love a stripclub owner possessed
Outran the pauser, reason. Here lay Kennedy

Act 2, Scene 3

His silver skin pierced by powerful bullets
And his ghastly head wounds look'd like a breach in nature
Jackie hopelessly stretching out to grasp
A slip'ry fragment of her husband's head.

When this cold murderer came down the Courthouse hallway
Harried along in the arms of Dallas deputies and
Homicide detectives, jack Ruby's heart could not refrain
And from it sprang forth the Courage to make his deep love
And respect for the First Lady known to her and the world.

Lady MacCain

Help me hence, ho!

Bobby Kennedy

Look to the lady.

Bobby Kennedy

[Aside to Ted Kennedy]
Why do we hold our tongues,
That most may claim this argument for ours?

Ted Kennedy

[Aside to Bobby Kennedy]
What should be spoken here,
where our fate, did in a manhole,
may rush, and seize us?
Let 's away;
Our tears are not yet brew'd.

Bobby Kennedy

[Aside to Ted Kennedy]
Nor our strong sorrow
Upon the foot of motion.

Colby

Look to the lady:
Lady MacCain is carried out
And when we have our naked frailties hid,
That suffer in exposure, let us meet,
And question this most bloody piece of work,
To know it further. Fears and scruples shake us:
In the great hand of God I stand; and thence
Against the undivulged pretence I fight
Of treasonous malice.

Bobby Kennedy

And so do I.

All

So all.

MacCain

Let's briefly put on manly readiness,
And meet the press in a conference.

All

Well contented.

Exeunt all but Bob Kennedy and Martin Luther King...

Bobby Kennedy

What will you do? Let's not consort with them:
To show an unfelt sorrow is an office
Which the false man does easy. I'll to Hyannisport.

Martin Luther King

To Birmingham, I; our separated fortune
Shall keep us both the safer: where we are,
There's daggers in men's smiles:

Bobby Kennedy

The right way hath not yet lighted, the safest
Is to avoid the aim. Therefore, to private jet;
And let us not be dainty of leave-taking,
But shift away: there's warrant in that theft
Which steals itself, when there's no mercy left.

Exeunt

Act 2 Scene 4

Outside MacCain's Penthouse

Enter Uncle Sam, Malcolm X and Joe Citizen...

Uncle Sam

Threescore and ten I can remember well:
Within the volume of which time I have seen
Hours dreadful and things strange;
But this sore night Hath trifled former knowings.

Malcolm X

Ah, good father, Thou seest, the heavens, as troubled with
man's act,
Threaten his bloody stage: by the clock, 'tis day
And yet dark night strangles the travelling lamp:
Is't night's predominance, or the day's shame,
That darkness does the face of earth entomb,
When living light should kiss it?

Uncle Sam

'Tis unnatural,
Even like the deed that's done. On Tuesday last,
A falcon, towering in her pride of place,
Was by a mousing owl hawk'd at and kill'd.

Malcolm X

And Kennedy's vintage autos — a thing most strange and
certain — Beauteous and swift, the minions of their race,
Turn'd wild in nature, broke their garages, spun out,
Contending 'gainst obedience,

Act 2, Scene 4

As they would make War with mankind.

Joe Citizen

'Tis said they crashed into each other.

Uncle Sam

They did so, to the amazement of mine eyes
That look'd upon't. Here comes good Lady Liberty.

   Enter Lady Liberty

How goes the world, madam, now?

Lady Liberty

Why, see you not?

Uncle Sam

Is't known who did this more than bloody deed?

Joe Citizen

Lee Harvey Oswald.

Uncle Sam

Alas, the day!
What good could he pretend?

Uncle Sam

He was compromised, having a secret history.
Bobby and Ted, the President's two brothers
Are stol'n away and fled; which puts upon them
The appearance of opposing the usurpers.

Lady Liberty

'Gainst nature still!
Thriftless ambition, that wilt ravin up
Thine own life's means! Then 'tis most like
The Presidency will come to fall upon MacCain.

58

Uncle Sam

He is already named, and gone to Arizona
To meet with his campaign contributors.

Lady Liberty

Where is the President's body?

Uncle Sam

Carried to an operating theatre in Parkland Hospital
And from there presently to Airforce One
From there apparently to the sacred storehouse of his predecessors,
And guardian of their bones.

Lady Liberty

Will you to Washington?

Uncle Sam

No, cousin, I'll to New York.

Lady Liberty

Well, I will thither.

Malcolm X

The future belongs to those who prepared for today.

Uncle Sam

Well, may you see things well done there: adieu!
Lest our old suits and ties sit easier than our new!

Lady Liberty

Farewell, father.

Joe Citizen

God's benison go with you; and with those
That would make good of bad, and friends of foes!

Exeunt

Act 3, Scene 1

MacCain's Luxury Apartment

Enter William Colby...

Colby

Thou hast it now: all,
As the weird women promised, and, I fear,
Thou play'dst most foully for't: yet it was said
It should not stand in thy posterity,
But that myself should be the root and father
Of many kings. If there come truth from them—
As upon thee, MacCain, their speeches shine—
Why, by the verities on thee made good,
May they not be my oracles as well,
And set me up in hope? But hush! no more.

Sennet sounded.

*Enter MacCain and Lady MacCain. In attendance are Edward
Lansdale, David Sánchez Morales, Oliver North, Donald Gregg,
Edmund Wilson, Richard Secord, Felix Rodríguez, Barry Seal,
Thomas Clines, Rafael Quintero, Ricardo Chavez and Bernard
Baker*

MacCain

Here's our chief guest.

Lady MacCain

If he had been forgotten,

It had been as a gap in our great feast,
And all-thing unbecoming.

MacCain

To-night we hold a solemn supper sir,
And I'll request your attendance.

Colby

Let your eminence
Command upon me; to the which my duties
Are with a most indissoluble tie
For ever knit.

MacCain

Drive you this afternoon?

Colby

Ay, my good lord.

MacCain

We should have else desired your good advice,
Which still hath been both grave and prosperous,
In this day's council; but we'll take to-morrow.
Is't far you drive to the East Coast of Maryland?

Colby

As far, my lord, as will fill up the time
'Twixt this and supper: go not my Lexus the better,
I must become a borrower of the night
For a dark hour or twain.

MacCain

Fail not our feast.

Colby

My lord, I will not.

MacCain

We hear, our bloody cousins are bestow'd
In Hyannisport and Birmingham, not confessing
Their cruel coolness to us, filling their hearers
With strange invention: but of that to-morrow,
When therewithal we shall have cause of state
Craving us jointly. Hie you to highway: adieu,
Till you return at night. Goes Shackley with you?

Colby

Ay, my good lord: our time does call upon 't.

MacCain

I wish your high-torque cylinders swiftness and
So I do commend you to their velocity. Farewell.

Exit Colby...

Let every man be master of his time
Till seven at night: to make society
The sweeter welcome, we will keep ourself
Till supper-time alone: then, God be with you!

Exit all but MacCain, and a security staffer...

Sirrah, a word with you:
Attend those men our pleasure?

Attendant

They are, my lord,
Waiting in the downstairs lobby.

MacCain

Bring them before us.

Exit Security Staffer...

To be thus is nothing; But to be safely thus

— Our fears in Colby stick deep;
And in his royalty of nature
Reigns that which would be fear'd: 'tis much he dares;
And, to that dauntless temper of his mind,
He hath a wisdom that doth guide his valour
To act in safety. There is none but he
Whose being I do fear: and, under him,
My Genius is rebuked; as, it is said,
Mark Antony's was by Caesar.
He chid the sisters
When first they put the name of President upon me,
And bade them speak to him:
Then prophet-like
They hail'd him father to a line of kings:
Upon my head they placed a fruitless crown,
And put a barren sceptre in my grip,
Thence to be wrench'd with an unreal hand,
No son of mine succeeding.
No young MacCain.
If 't be so, For Banquo's issue have I filled my mind;
For them the gracious Kennedy have I murder'd;
Put rancours in the vessel of my peace
Only for them; and mine eternal jewel
Given to the common enemy of man,
To make the seed of Colby kings!
Rather than so, come fate into the list.
And champion me to the utterance!
Who's there!

Re-enter Attendant,
with two Operation Phoenix Assassins

Now go to the door,
and stay there till we call.

Exit Attendant...

Was it not yesterday we spoke together?

Clines

It was, so please your eminence...

MacCain

Well then, now
Have you consider'd of my speeches?
Know that it was he in the times past which held you
So under fortune, which you thought had been
Our innocent self: this I made good to you
In our last conference, pass'd in probation with you,
How you were borne in hand, how cross'd, the instruments,
Who wrought with them, and all things else that might to half
a soul and to a notion crazed say: '*Thus did Colby.*'

Felix Rodríguez

You made it known to us.

MacCain

I did so, and went further, which is now
Our point of second meeting. Do you find
patience so predominant in your nature
That you can let this go? Are you so gospell'd
To pray for this good man and for his issue,
Whose heavy hand hath bow'd you to the grave
And beggar'd yours for ever? You are going to be
the equivalent of a beat cop forever, do you get it?

Clines

We are men, my liege.

MacCain

Ay, in the catalogue ye go for men;
As hounds and greyhounds, mongrels, spaniels, curs,

65

Act 3, Scene 1

Shoughs, water-rugs and demi-wolves, are clept
All by the name of dogs: the valued file
Distinguishes the swift, the slow, the subtle,
The housekeeper, the hunter, every one
According to the gift which bounteous nature
Hath in him closed; whereby he does receive
Particular addition from the bill
That writes them all alike: and so of men.
Now, if you have a station in the file,
Not i' the worst rank of manhood, say 't;
And I will put that business in your bosoms,
Whose execution takes your enemy off,
Grapples you to the heart and love of us,
Who wear our health but sickly in his life,
Which in his death were perfect.

Clines

I am one, my liege,
Whom the vile blows and buffets of the world
Have so incensed that I am reckless what
I do to spite the world.

Felix Rodríguez

And I another
So weary with disasters, tugg'd with fortune,
That I would set my lie on any chance,
To mend it, or be rid on't.

MacCain

Both of you
Know Colby was your enemy.

Both Murderers

True, my lord.

MacCain

So is he mine; and in such bloody distance,
That every minute of his being thrusts
Against my near'st of life: and though I could
With barefaced power sweep him from my sight
And bid my will avouch it, yet I must not,
For certain friends that are both his and mine,
Whose loves I may not drop, but wail his fall
Who I myself struck down; and thence it is,
That I to your assistance make avail,
Masking the business from the common eye
For sundry weighty reasons.

Clines

We shall, sir,
Perform what you command us.

Felix Rodríguez

Though our lives —

MacCain

Your spirits shine through you.
Within this hour at most
I will advise you of the GPS
and where to station yourselves;
Acquaint you with the perfect spy o' the time,
The moment on't; for't must be done to-night,
And something from the palace; always thought
That I require a clearness: and with him—
To leave no rubs nor botches in the work—
Shackley, the blonde who keeps him company,
Whose absence is no less material to me
Than is his boss', also must embrace the fate
Of that dark hour. Resolve yourselves apart:

I'll come to you anon.

Both Assassins

We are resolved, my lord.

MacCain

I'll call upon you straight: abide within.

Exit Assassins...

It is concluded. Colby, thy soul's flight,
If it find heaven, must find it out to-night.

Exeunt

Act 3, Scene 2

The palace.

Enter Lady MacCain and a Servant...

Lady MacCain

Has Colby left his rooms?

Servant

Ay, madam, but returns again to-night.

Lady MacCain

Say to the king, I would attend his leisure
For a few words.

Servant

Madam, I will.

Exit Servant...

Lady MacCain

Nought's had, all's spent,
Where our desire is got without content:
'Tis safer to be that which we destroy
Than by destruction dwell in doubtful joy.

Enter MacCain...

How now, my lord! why do you keep alone,
Of sorriest fancies your companions making,

Act 2, Scene 3

Using those thoughts which should indeed have died with
them they think on?
Things without all remedy should be without regard: what's
done is done.

MacCain

We have scotch'd the snake, not kill'd it:
She'll close and be herself, whilst our poor malice
Remains in danger of her former tooth.
But let the frame of things disjoint,
Both the worlds suffer,
Ere we will eat our meal in fear and sleep
In the affliction of these terrible dreams
That shake us nightly: better be with the dead,
Whom we, to gain our peace, have sent to peace,
Than on the torture of the mind to lie
In restless ecstasy. Kennedy is in his grave;
After life's fitful fever he sleeps well;
Treason has done his worst: nor steel, nor poison,
Malice domestic, foreign threats, nothing,
Can touch him further.

Lady MacCain

Come on;
Gentle my lord, sleek o'er your rugged looks;
Be bright and jovial among your guests to-night.

MacCain

So shall I, love; and so, I pray, be you:
Let your remembrance apply to Colby;
Present him eminence, both with eye and tongue:
Unsafe the while, that we must lave our honours in these
flattering streams, And make our faces vizards to our hearts,
Disguising what they are.

Lady MacCain

You must leave this.

MacCain

O, full of scorpions is my mind, dear wife!
Thou know'st that Colby, and his Shackley, live.

Lady MacCain

But nature did not make them eternal.

MacCain

There's comfort yet; they are assailable;
You joke around then: ere the bat hath flown
His cloister'd flight to black Hecate's summons
Ere the shard-borne beetle with his drowsy hums
Hath rung night's yawning peal,
There shall be done a deed of dreadful note.

Lady MacCain

What's to be done?

MacCain

Be innocent of the knowledge, dearest chipmunk,
Till thou applaud the deed. Come, the seal of night,
Scarfs up the tender eye of pitiful day;
And with thy bloody and invisible hand
Cancel and tear to pieces that great bond
Which keeps me pale! Light thickens;
And the crow makes wing to the rooky wood:
Good things of day begin to droop and drowse;
While night's black agents to their preys do rouse.
Thou marvell'st at my words: but hold thee still;
Things bad begun make strong themselves by ill.
So, prithee, go with me.

Exeunt

Act 3 Scene 3
Colby's Cottage

Enter three Assassins...

Clines
But who did bid thee join with us?

Sturgis
MacCain

Felix Rodríguez
He needs not our mistrust, since he delivers
Our offices and what we have to do
To the direction just.

Clines
Then stand with us.
The west yet glimmers with some streaks of day:
Now to gain the timely cabin; and make near approaches to
the subject of our watch.

Felix Rodríguez
Hark! I hear footsteps

Colby
[Within] Turn on the light, Ted!

Clines
Then 'tis he: the rest
That are within the note of expectation

Act 3, Scene 3

Already are i' the court.

Sturgis
They are walking about.

Felix Rodríguez
He does usually, as some men do...

Clines
Be alert. Let's not get caught with our pants down.

Enter Colby, and Shackley with a flashlight...

Felix Rodríguez
'Tis he.

Clines
Get ready.

Colby
It will be rain to-night.

Sturgis
Let it come down.

They subdue and inject Colby...

Banquo
O, treachery! Fly, good Theodore, fly, fly, fly!
Thou mayst revenge. O you mercenary villain!

Goes unconscious. Shackley escapes...

Clines
Who did strike out the light?

Felix Rodríguez

Wast not the way?

Sturgis

There's but one down; the blonde is fled.

Clines

We have lost the best half of our affair.

Felix Rodríguez

Well, let's away, and say how much is done.

Exeunt

Act 3 Scene 4

The same. Hall in the Luxury Apartment

A banquet prepared. Enter MacCain, Lady MacCain, General Lyman Lemnitzer, General Curtis Lemay, Oliver North, Donald Gregg, Richard Secord, Charles Cabell, Washington Notables and Security Staffers

MacCain

You know your own degrees; sit down: at first
And last the hearty welcome.

Lords

Thanks to your majesty.

MacCain

Ourself will mingle with society,
And play the humble host.
Our hostess keeps her state, but in best time
We will require her welcome.

Lady MacCain

Pronounce it for me, sir, to all our friends;
For my heart speaks they are welcome.

First Assassin appears at the door...

MacCain

See, they encounter thee with their hearts' thanks.
Both sides are even: here I'll sit i' the midst:

Act 3, Scene 4

Be large in mirth; anon we'll drink a measure
The table round.
Approaching the door
There's blood on thy face.

Sturgis

'Tis Colby's then. He hit his head.

MacCain

Is he dispatch'd?

Felix Rodríguez

My lord, he is drowned, that I did for him.

MacCain

Thou art the best o' the waterboarders: yet he's good
That did the like for Shackley: if thou didst it,
Thou art unequalled among assassins.

Clines

Most royal sir, Shackley is 'scaped.

MacCain

Here comes my fit again: I had else been perfect,
Whole as the marble, founded as the rock,
As broad and general as the refreshing air:
But now I am cabin'd, cribb'd, confined, bound in
To saucy doubts and fears. But Colby's safe?

Sturgis

Ay, my good lord: safe in his canoe he bides,
With only a nasty gash where he hit his head
The least a death to nature.

MacCain

Thanks for that:

There the grown serpent lies; the worm that's fled
Hath nature that in time will venom breed,
No teeth for the present.
Get thee gone: to-morrow
We'll hear, ourselves, again.

Exit Murderer...

Lady MacCain

My royal lord,
You do not give the cheer: the feast is old
That is not often vouch'd, while 'tis a-making,
'Tis given with welcome: to feed were best at home;
From thence the sauce to meat is ceremony;
Meeting were bare without it.

MacCain

Sweet remembrancer!
Now, good digestion wait on appetite,
And health on both!

Gregg

May't please your highness sit.

The ghost of Colby enters, and sits in MacCain's place...

MacCain

Here had we now our country's honour roof'd,
Were the graced person of our Colby present;
Who may I rather challenge for unkindness
Than pity for mischance!

Freidman

His absence, sir,
Lays blame upon his promise.

Act 3, Scene 4

Please't your highness
To grace us with your royal company.

MacCain

The table's full.

Gregg

Here is a place reserved, sir.

MacCain

Where?

General Lemnitzer

Here, my good lord. What is't that moves your highness?

MacCain

Which of you have done this?

Lords

What, my good lord?

MacCain

Thou canst not say I did it: never shake
Thy gory locks at me.

Lemay

Gentlemen, rise: his highness is not well.

Lady MacCain

Sit, worthy friends: my lord is often thus,
on account of his war wounds: pray you, keep seat;
The fit is momentary; upon a thought
He will again be well: if much you note him,
You shall offend him and extend his passion:
Feed, and regard him not. Are you a man?

MacCain

Ay, and a bold one, that dare look on that
Which might appal the devil.

Lady MacCain

O proper stuff!
This is the very painting of your fear:
This is the phantom sniper rifles which, you said,
Led you to dead Kennedy. O, these flaws and starts,
Impostors to true fear, would well become
A woman's story at a winter's fire,
Authorized by her grandam. Shame itself!
Why do you make such faces? When all's done,
You look but on a stool.

MacCain

Prithee, see there! behold! look! lo!
how say you?
Why, what care I? If thou canst nod, speak too.
If charnel-houses and our graves must send
Those that we bury back, our monuments
Shall be inside the mouths of sea birds.

Ghost of Colby vanishes...

Lady MacCain

What, quite unmann'd in folly?

MacCain

If I stand here, I saw him.

Lady MacCain

Fie, for shame!

Act 3, Scene 4

MacCain

Blood hath been shed ere now, i' the olden time,
Ere human statute purged the gentle weal;
Ay, and since too, murders have been perform'd
Too terrible for the ear: the times have been,
That, when the brains were out, the man would die,
And there an end; but now they rise again,
With twenty mortal murders on their crowns,
And push us from our stools: this is more strange
Than such a murder is.

Lady MacCain

My worthy lord,
Your noble friends don't get you.

MacCain

I do forget.
Do not muse at me, my most worthy friends,
I have post traumatic shock syndrome, which is nothing
To those that know me. Come, love and health to all;
Then I'll sit down. Give me some wine; fill full.
I drink to the general joy o' the whole table,
And to our dear friend Colby, whom we miss;
Would he were here! to all, and him, we thirst,
And all to all.

Lords

Our duties, and the pledge.

Re-enter Ghost of Colby...

MacCain

Avaunt! and quit my sight! let the earth hide thee!
Thy bones are marrowless, thy blood is cold;
Thou hast no speculation in those eyes

Which thou dost glare with!

Lady MacCain

Think of this, good peers,
But as a flashback: 'tis no other;
Only it spoils the pleasure of the time.

MacCain

What man dare, I dare:
Approach thou like the rugged Russian bear,
The arm'd rhinoceros, or the ferocious tiger;
Take any shape but that, and my firm nerves
Shall never tremble: or be alive again,
And dare me to the desert with thy sword;
If trembling I inhabit then, protest me
The baby of a girl. Hence, horrible shadow!
Unreal mockery, Hollywood monster, hence!

   Ghost of Colby vanishes...

Why, so: being gone,
I am a man again. Pray you, sit still.

Lady MacCain

You have displaced the mirth, broke the good meeting,
With most admired disorder. You should not take LSD.

MacCain

Can such things be,
And overcome us like a summer's cloud,
Without our noticing what has happened?
You make me strange
Even to my own peculiar nature,
When now I think you can behold such sights,
And keep the color of your cheeks,
When mine are blanched with fear.

Act 3, Scene 4

Donald Gregg

What sights, my lord?

Lady MacCain

I pray you, speak not;
His nervous condition grows worse and worse;
Questions enrage him.
At once, good night:
It was his experience in the tiger cages of Vietnam that has
From time to time unhinged him.
Stand not upon the order of your going,
But go at once.

Freidman

Good night; and better health
Attend his majesty!

Lady MacCain

A kind good night to all!

   Exit all but MacCain and Lady MacCain...

MacCain

It will have blood; they say, blood will have blood:
Stones have been known to move and trees to speak;
Profilers and forensic experts reconstruct relations
By magot-pies and lungs and swabs brought forth
The secret'st man of blood. What is the night?

Lady MacCain

Almost at odds with morning, which is which.

MacCain

How say'st thou, that Bobby Kennedy denies his person
At our great bidding?

Lady MacCain

Did you send to him, John?

MacCain

I hear it by the way; but I will send:
There's not a one of them but in his house
I keep a servant fee'd. I will to-morrow,
And betimes I will, to the weird sisters:
More shall they speak; for now I am bent to know,
By the worst means, the worst. For mine own good,
All causes shall give way: I am in blood
Stepp'd in so far that, should I wade no more,
Returning were as tedious as go o'er:
Strange things I have in head, that will to hand;
Which must be acted ere they may be scann'd.

Lady MacCain

You lack the season of all natures, sleep.

MacCain

Come, we'll to sleep. My strange and self-abuse
Is the initiate fear that wants hard use:
Bring the whips, we are yet but young in deed.

Exeunt

Act 3 Scene 5
A Jungle Clearing

Thunder. Enter the three Witches meeting Hecate

First Witch

Why, how now, Hecate! You look angerly.

Hecate

Have I not reason, bedlams as you are,
Saucy and overbold? In the future you
Better stick to your pseudo-philosophies
How did you dare
To trade and traffic with MacCain
In riddles and affairs of death;
And I, the mistress of your charms,
The close contriver of all harms,
Was never call'd to bear my part,
Or show the glory of our art?
And, which is worse, all you have done
Hath been but for a wayward son,
Spiteful and wrathful, who, as others do,
Loves for his own ends, not for you.
But make amends now: get you gone,
To hidden graves of Iguala by dawn.
Meet me i' the morning: thither he
Will come to know his destiny:
Your vessels and your spells provide,
Your charms and every thing beside.
I am for the air; this night I'll spend
Unto a dismal and a fatal end:

Great business must be wrought ere noon:
Upon the corner of the moon
In an Operation Paperclip studio
There hangs a vaporous drop profound;
I'll catch it ere it come to ground:
And that distill'd by magic sleights
In an MK-Ultra chemistry laboratory
I shall raise such artificial sprites
As by the strength of their illusion
Shall draw him on to his confusion:
He shall spurn fate, scorn death, and bear
He hopes 'bove wisdom, grace and fear:
And you all know, security
Is mortals' chiefest enemy.

Leadbelly Mississippi Blues Music and a song within:

'Come away, come away,' &
Hark! I am call'd; my little spirit, see,
Sits in a foggy cloud, and stays for me.

First Witch

Come, let's make haste; she'll soon be back again.

Exeunt

Act 3 Scene 6
Washington. The White House

Enter Lyndon Johnson and Edward Landsdale

Lyndon Johnson
My former speeches have but hit your thoughts,
Which can interpret further: only, I say,
Things have been strangely borne.
The gracious John Kennedy
Was pitied of MacCain: marry, he was dead:
And the right-valiant Colby walk'd too late;
Whom, you may say, if't please you, Shackley kill'd,
For Shackley fled: men must not walk too late
or go about in a canoe when the wind is blown.
Who cannot want the thought how monstrous
It was for Bobby Kennedy and for Martin Luther King
To diss the new political establishment? Damned fact!
How it did grieve MacCain! Did he not straight
In pious rage call for the death penalty for regicides
When they are Fair Play For Cuba committee members?
Was not that nobly done? Ay, and wisely too;
For 'twould have anger'd any heart alive
To hear the men deny't. So that, I say,
He has borne all things well: and I do think
That had he has Kennedy's brothers under his key—
As, an't please heaven, he shall not—they should find
What 'twere to kill a father; so should Shackley.
But, peace! for from broad words and 'cause he fail'd

Act 3, Scene 6

His presence at the tyrant's feast, I hear
Bobby Kennedy is in hiding: sir, can you tell
Where he bestows himself?

Edward Lansdale

The brother of the late President,
From whom this punk holds the due of birth
Lives in Hyannisport and is received
By the credulous New Englanders
And the unwashed Popish voters
Of Irish, Italian, and Polish descent.
That the malevolence of fortune nothing
Takes from his high respect: thither Bobby Kennedy
Is gone to pray the holy king Joe upon his aid
To wake the scions of liberal establishment
That, by the help of these—with Him above
To ratify the work—we may again
Give to our tables meat, sleep to our nights,
With the defense contracts on a steady growing pace
Free from our feasts and banquets bloody knives,
Do faithful homage and receive medals of honours:
All which we pine for now: and this report
Hath so exasperated the Democrats that
A mousey professor in a state university
Has prepared for some attempt of war.

Lyndon Johnson

Sent he to Bobby Kennedy?

Edward Lansdale

He did: and with an absolute *'Sir, not I,'*
The cloudy messenger turns me his back,
And hums, as who should say *'You'll rue the time
That clogs me with this answer.'*

Lyndon Johnson

And that well might
Advise him to a caution, to hold what distance
His wisdom can provide. Some holy angel
Fly to the national campaign headquarters and unfold
His message ere he come, that a swift blessing
May soon return to this our suffering country
Under a hand accursed!

Edward Lansdale

I'll send my prayers with him.

Exeunt

Act 4 Scene 1

A cavern. In the middle, a boiling cauldron.

Thunder. Enter the three Witches

First Witch

Thrice the brinded cat hath mew'd.

Second Witch

Thrice and once the hedge-pig whined.

Third Witch

Harpier cries 'Tis time, 'tis time.

First Witch

Round about the cauldron go;
In the poison'd entrails throw.
Toad, that under cold stone
Days and nights has thirty-one
Swelter'd venom sleeping got,
Boil thou first i' the charmed pot.

All

Double, double toil and trouble;
Fire burn, and cauldron bubble.

Second Witch

Fillet of a fenny snake,
In the cauldron boil and bake;
Eye of newt and toe of frog,
Wool of bat and tongue of dog,

Act 4, Scene 1

Adder's fork and blind-worm's sting,
Lizard's leg and owlet's wing,
For a charm of powerful trouble,
Like a hell-broth boil and bubble.

All

Double, double toil and trouble;
Fire burn and cauldron bubble.

Third Witch

Scale of dragon, tooth of wolf,
Witches' mummy, oil pressed
from the ravin'd salt-sea shark,
Root of hemlock digg'd i' the dark,
Liver of blaspheming Jew,
Gall of goat, and slips of yew
Silver'd in the moon's eclipse,
Nose of Turk and Tartar's lips,
Finger of birth-strangled babe
Ditch-deliver'd
Making the gruel thick and greasy
For the ingredients of our cauldron.

All

Double, double toil and trouble;
Fire burn and cauldron bubble.

Second Witch

Cool it with a baboon's blood,
Then the charm is firm and good.

Enter Hecate to the other three Witches...

Hecate

O well done! I commend your pains;
And every one shall share i' the gains;

And now about the cauldron sing,
Live elves and fairies in a ring,
Enchanting all that you put in.

Old Mississippi Blues Music and a song: 'Black Spirits'
Hecate retires...

Second Witch

By the pricking of my thumbs,
Something wicked this way comes.
Open, locks,
Whoever knocks!

Enter MacCain...

MacCain

How now, you secret, black, and midnight hags!
What is't you do?

All

A deed without a name.

MacCain

I conjure you, by that which you profess,
Howe'er you come to know it, answer me:
Though you untie the winds and let them fight
Against the churches; though the feisty waves
Confound and swallow navigation up;
Though bladed corn be lodged in the hedges and trees blown
down;
Though office buildings topple on the heads of the lease
holders;
Though presidential palaces fall to color revolutions
of the Ford and Rockefeller and Heritage foundations; though
the treasure

Of the defense, drugs, petroleum and banking industries
tumble all together,
Even till destruction sicken; answer me
To what I ask you.

First Witch

Speak.

Second Witch

Demand.

Third Witch

We'll answer.

First Witch

Say, if thou'dst rather hear it from our mouths,
Or from our masters?

MacCain

Call 'em; let me see 'em.

First Witch

Pour in some pig's blood, that hath eaten
Her nine piglets; grease that's sweatened
by the chaplain from the murderer's brow
— Into the flame.

All

Come, high or low;
Thyself and your position deftly show!

Thunder. First Apparition: an armed Head...

MacCain

Tell me, thou unknown power,—

First Witch

He knows thy thought:
Hear his speech, but don't speak yourself.

First Apparition

MacCain! MacCain! MacCain! Beware of Kennedy;
Beware Beware of Joe's sons. Dismiss me. Enough.

Descends...

MacCain

Whate'er thou art, for thy good caution, thanks;
Thou hast harp'd my fear aright:
But one word more,—

First Witch

He will not be commanded: here's another,
More potent than the first.

Thunder. Second Apparition: A bloody child...

Second Apparition

MacCain! MacCain! MacCain!

MacCain

Had I three ears, I'd hear thee.

Second Apparition

Be bloody, bold, and resolute; laugh to scorn
The power of man, for none of dame born
Shall harm MacCain.

Descends...

MacCain

Then live, Kennedy: what need I fear of thee?
Everyone knows your mother's name is Rose.
But yet I'll make assurance double sure,
And take a bond of fate: thou shalt never again live;
That I may tell pale-hearted fear it lies,
And sleep in spite of thunder.

> *Thunder...*
> *Third Apparition: a child crowned, with a tree in his hand...*

What is this
That rises like the issue of a king,
And wears upon his baby-brow the round
And top of sovereignty?

All

Listen, but speak not to't.

Third Apparition

Be lion-mettled, proud; and take no care
Who chafes, who frets, or where conspirers are:
MacCain shall never vanquish'd be until
Central Park comes up to his Penthouse.

> *Descends...*

MacCain

That will never be
Who can impress the forest, bid the tree
Unfix his earth-bound root? Sweet bodements! Good!
Rebellion's head, rise never till the wood
Of Central Park rise, and our high-placed MacCain
Shall live the life of luxury, pay his breath
To time and mortal custom. Yet my heart
Throbs to know one thing: tell me, if your art

Can tell so much: shall Colby's issue then
Reign in this kingdom?

All

Seek to know no more.

MacCain

I will be satisfied: deny me this,
And an eternal curse fall on you! Let me know.
Why sinks that cauldron? And what noise is this?
Hautboys

First Witch

Show!

Second Witch

Show!

Third Witch

Show!

All

Show his eyes, and grieve his heart;
Come like shadows, so depart!

> *A show of Assassinated US Presidents, the last with a glass in his hand; Ghost of Colby following...*

MacCain

Thou art too like the spirit of Banquo: down!
Thy crown does sear mine eye-balls. And thy hair,
Thou other gold-bound brow, is like the first.
A third is like the former. Filthy hags!
Why do you show me this? A fourth! Start, eyes!
What, will the line stretch out to the crack of doom?
Another yet! A seventh! I'll see no more:

Act 4, Scene 1

And yet the eighth appears, who bears a glass
Which shows me many more; and some I see
That two-fold balls and treble scepters carry:
Horrible sight! Now, I see, 'tis true;
For the blood-bolter'd Colby smiles upon me,
And points at them for his.

Apparitions of assassinated US Presidents vanish

What, is this so?

First Witch

Ay, sir, all this is so: but why
Stands MacCain thus amazedly?
Come, sisters, cheer we up his spirits,
And show the best of our delights:
I'll charm the air to give a sound,
While you perform your antic round:
That this great king may kindly say,
Our duties did his welcome pay.

Music. The witches dance and then vanish, with Hecate...

MacCain

Where are they? Gone? Let this pernicious hour
Stand aye accursed in the calendar!
Come in, without there!

Enter Shackley...

Shackley

What's your grace's will?

MacCain

Saw you the weird sisters?

Shackley

No, my lord.

MacCain

They didn't pass you?

Shackley

No, indeed, my lord.

MacCain

Infected be the air whereon they ride;
And damn'd all those that trust them! I did hear
The sound of an automobile: who was't came by?

Shackley

'Tis two or three, my lord, that bring you word
That the Ghost of JFK is fled to a safe house.

MacCain

Fled to a safe house!

Shackley

Ay, my good lord.

MacCain

Time, thou anticipatest my dread exploits:
The flighty purpose never is o'ertook
Unless the deed go with it; from this moment
The very firstlings of my heart shall be
The firstlings of my hand. And even now,
To crown my thoughts with acts, be it thought and done:
The resort houses of Kennedy I will surprise;
Seize upon Hyannis; give to the edge o' the sword
His wife, his babes, and all unfortunate souls
That trace him in his line. No boasting like a fool;
This deed I'll do before this purpose cools.
But no more sights! —Where are these gentlemen
With fresh news? Come, bring me where they are.

Exeunt

Act 4 Scene 2

Inside the Statue of Liberty

Enter Lady Liberty her Son, and Uncle Sam

Lady Liberty

Why had those teams of cruel assassins been activated?

Uncle Sam

You must have patience, lady.

Lady Liberty

He had none:
Our fears do make us traitors.

Uncle Sam

You know not
Whether he was pushed by wisdom or fear

Lady Liberty

Wisdom?
To leave Hyannisport
or to be safe in Camp David?
His privileged lifestyle, his position
To risk it just like that.
Why did he ever take that fateful trip?

Uncle Sam

My dearest, coz,

Lady Liberty

I'm asking you to get a hold of yourself: since your husband,
He is noble, wise, judicious, and best knows
The fits o' the season. It's better if I won't say more;
But cruel are the times, when we are traitors
And fail to know ourselves, when we hold secrets
From what we fear, without really knowing what we fear of
But float upon a wild and violent sea
Without knowing where it will take us. I have to leave now:
Shall not be long but I'll be here again:
Things will get better, or maybe not
As this happened before. My pretty cousin,
Blessing upon you!

Lady Liberty, cries

Brother he is, yet he is brotherless!

Bobby Kennedy

With what I get, I deal; and so do they.

Lady Liberty

Poor bird! thou'ldst never fear the net nor lime,
The pitfall nor the gin.

Bobby Kennedy

Why should I, mother? Poor birds they are not set for.
My brother is not really dead, for all your saying.

Lady Liberty

Yes, he is dead; how wilt thou do for a brother?

Bobby Kennedy

Nay, how will you do for a husband?

Lady Liberty

Why, I can buy me twenty at any market.

Bobby Kennedy

Then you'll buy 'em to sell again.

Lady Liberty

Thou speak'st with all thy wit: and yet, i' faith,
With wit enough for thee.

Bobby Kennedy

Was my father a traitor, mother?

Lady Liberty

Ay, that he was.

Bobby Kennedy

What is a traitor?

Lady Liberty

Why, one that swears and lies.

Bobby Kennedy

And be all traitors that do so?

Lady Liberty

Every one that does so is a traitor, and must be hanged.

Bobby Kennedy

And must they all be hanged that swear and lie?

Lady Liberty

Every one.

Bobby Kennedy

Who must hang them?

Act 4, Scene 2

Lady Liberty

Why, the honest men.

Bobby Kennedy

Then the liars and swearers are fools,
for there are liars and swearers enough to beat
the honest men and hang up them.

Lady Liberty

Now, God help thee, poor monkey!
But how wilt thou do for a father?

Bobby Kennedy

If he were dead, you'd weep for
him: if you would not, it were a good sign
that I should quickly have a new father.

Lady Liberty

Poor prattler, how thou talk'st!

Enter a Messenger...

Joe Citizen

Bless you, fair dame! I am not to you known,
Though in your state of honour I am perfect.
I doubt some danger does approach you nearly:
If you will take a homely man's advice,
Be not found here; hence, with your little ones.
To fright you thus, methinks, I am too savage;
To do worse to you were fell cruelty,
Which is too nigh your person. Heaven preserve you!
I dare abide no longer.

Exit Joe Citizen

Lady Liberty

Whither should I fly?
I have done no harm. But I remember now
I am in this earthly world; where to do harm
Is often laudable, to do good sometime
Accounted dangerous folly: why then, alas,
Do I put up that womanly defence,
To say I have done no harm?

> *Enter girl in a polka dot dress with Sirhan Sirhan. Bodyguards
> with sunglasses and walkie talkies...*

What are these faces?

> *Enter Assassins...*

David Morales

Where is your husband?

Lady MacCain

I hope, in no place so unsanctified
Where such as thou mayst find him.

Gordon Campbell

He's a traitor.

Bobby Kennedy

Thou liest, thou shag-hair'd villain!

David Morales

What, you egg!
Body guard shoots him in the back of his head.
Young fry of treachery!

Bobby Kennedy

He has kill'd me, mother:
Run away, I pray you!

> *Dies*
> *Exeunt Assassins and Bodyguards.*
> *Exeunt the Girl in the Polka Dot .*
> *Exeunt Lady Liberty crying 'Murder!'.*
> *She flees down the Holland Tunnel to New Jersey.*

Act 4 Scene 3

Washington. Before the White House.

Enter Joe Citizen and The Ghost of John Kennedy

The Ghost of John Kennedy

Let us seek out some desolate shade, and there
Weep our sad bosoms empty.

Joe Citizen

Let us rather
Hold fast the mortal sword, and like good men
Bestride our down-fall'n birthdom: each new morn
New widows howl, new orphans cry, new sorrows
Strike heaven on the face, that it resounds
As if it felt with the United States of America and yell'd out
Like a syllable of pain.

The Ghost of John Kennedy

What I believe I'll wail,
What know believe, and what I can redress,
As I shall find the time undertake, I will.
What you have spoke, it may be so perchance.
This tyrant, whose sole name blisters our tongues,
Was once thought honest: you have loved him well.
He hath not touch'd you yet. I am young; but something
You may deserve of him through me, and wisdom
To offer up a weak poor innocent lamb
To appease an angry god.

Act 4, Scene 3

Joe Citizen

I am not treacherous.

The Ghost of John Kennedy

But MacCain is.
A good and virtuous nature may recoil
In an imperial charge.
But I shall crave your pardon;
That which you are my thoughts cannot transpose:
Angels are bright still, though the brightest fell;
Though all things foul would wear the brows of grace,
Yet grace can never change her good looks.

Joe Citizen

I have lost my hopes.

The Ghost of John Kennedy

Perchance even there where I did find my doubts.
Why in that rawness leave your native country,
Those precious motives, those strong knots of love,
Without I saying good-bye? I pray you,
Let not my revenge be your dishonour,
But my own legacy. After all, you may be rightly just,
Whatever I shall think.

Joe Citizen

Bleed, bleed, poor country!
Great tyranny! You are all set;
For goodness dare not check thee:
Though thy wrongs ye wear as clothes.
The office is smeared! Fare thee well, lord:
I would not be the villain that thou think'st
For the whole space that's in the tyrant's grasp,
And the poppy plantations of the East to boot.

The Ghost of John Kennedy

Be not offended:
I speak not as in absolute fear of you.
I think our country sinks beneath the yoke;
It weeps, it bleeds; and each new day a gash
Is added to her wounds: I think withal
There would be hands uplifted in my right;
And from the gracious common citizens
Have I been offered goodly millions: but, for all this,
When I shall tread upon the tyrant's head,
Or wear it on my sword, yet my poor country
Shall have more vices than it had before,
More suffering and in more ways than ever.

Joe Citizen

What do you mean?

The Ghost of John Kennedy

It is myself I mean: in whom I know
All the particulars of vice so grafted
That, when they shall be open'd, black MacCain
Will seem as pure as snow, and the poor state
Esteem him as a lamb, being compared
With my confineless harms secretely recorded
In those infernal houses of VIP prostitution.
Not in the legions
Of horrid hell can come a devil more damn'd
In evils to top MacCain.
I grant him bloody,
Luxurious, avaricious, false, deceitful,
Sudden, malicious, smacking of every sin
That has a name: but there's no bottom, none,
In my voluptuousness: your wives, your daughters,
Your matrons and your maids, could not fill up
The cistern of my lust, and my desire

Act 4, Scene 3

All continent impediments would o'erbear
That did oppose my will: better MacCain
Than such an one to reign.

Joe Citizen

Boundless intemperance
In nature is a tyranny; it hath been
The untimely emptying of the happy throne
And fall of many kings. But fear not yet
To take upon you what is yours: you may
Convey your pleasures in a spacious plenty,
And yet seem cold, the time you may so hoodwink.
We have willing gals enough: there cannot be
That vulture in you, to devour so many
As will to greatness dedicate themselves,
Finding it so inclined.

The Ghost of John Kennedy

With this there grows
In my most ill-composed affection such
A stanchless avarice that, were I President,
I should cut off the oil depletion allowance,
off shore banking and naked default swaps:
And my more-having would be as a sauce
To make me hunger more
Like Scrooge McDuck that I should forge
Quarrels unjust against the good and loyal,
by nationalizing the Federal Reserve Board
And destroying them for their wealth.

Joe Citizen

This avarice
Sticks deeper, grows with more pernicious root
Than summer-seeming lust, and it hath been
The sword of our slain Presidents: yet do not fear;
Wall Street hath instruments to fill up your will;

all these are portable, with other values added.

The Ghost of John Kennedy

But I have none of the king-becoming graces,
As justice, verity, temperance, stableness,
Bounty, perseverance, mercy, lowliness,
Devotion, patience, courage, fortitude,
I have no relish of them, but abound
In the division of each several crime,
Acting it many ways. Nay, had I power, I should
Pour the sweet milk of concord into hell,
Uproar the universal peace, confound
All unity on earth wreaking havoc on them.

Uncle Sam

O United States of America!
United States of America!

The Ghost of John Kennedy

If such a one be fit to govern, speak:
I am as I have spoken.

Uncle Sam

Fit to govern! Hardly. O nation miserable,
With an untitled tyrant bloody-scepter'd,
When shalt thou see thy wholesome days again,
Since that the truest issue of thy Presidency
By his own choleric testimony stands accursed,
And does blaspheme his entire family?
Your forefathers were inspired sages: the Constitution that
bore thee, Oftener upon her knees than on her feet,
Died every day she lived. Fare thee well!
These evils thou repeat'st upon thyself
Have banish'd me from the shores
and the waving grain of America.
O my breast, Thy hope ends here!

Act 4, Scene 3

The Ghost of John Kennedy

Sam, this noble passion,
Child of integrity, hath from my soul
Wiped the black scruples, reconciled my thoughts
To thy good truth and honour. Devilish MacCain
By many of these trains hath sought to win me
Into his power, and modest wisdom plucks me
From over-credulous haste: but God above
Deal between thee and me! For even now
I put myself to thy direction, and
Unspeak mine own detraction, here abjure
The taints and blames I laid upon myself,
For strangers to my nature. I have never yet
Know true love, and never was unfaithful as
Loyal Lady Liberty appears to me in dreams.
Scarcely have coveted what was mine own,
At no time broke my faith, would not betray
The devil to his fellow and delight
No less in truth than life: my first false speaking
Was this upon myself: what I am truly,
Is thine and my poor country's to command:
I learned my lesson that day in Dealy Plaza.
Whither indeed, before thy here-approach,
Old Left liberals, with ten thousands of scribes
Setting forth from remnants of the FDR coalition.
Now we'll together; and the chance of goodness
Be like our warranted quarrel! But why are you silent?

Joe Citizen

Such welcome and unwelcome things at once
'Tis hard to reconcile. Are you feeling well?

Enter Joe Citizen Junior...

The Ghost of John Kennedy

Well; more anon. —Comes your son forth, I pray you?

Joe Citizen Junior

Ay, sir; there are a crew of wretched souls
Abetting their addiction to power and deceit
Their malady convinces themselves but at his touch—
Such sanctity hath heaven given his hand—
They presently amend.

The Ghost of John Kennedy

I thank you, faithful patriot.

Exit Joe Citizen Junior...

Joe Citizen

What's the disease he means?

The Ghost of John Kennedy

'Tis call'd the evil:
A most miraculous work in the television;
Since I have been around Washington,
I have seen him heal viewers. How he solicits heaven,
Himself best knows: but strangely-visited people,
All swoln and ulcerous, pitiful to the eye,
The mere despair of surgery, he cures,
Hanging a golden stamp about their necks,
Put on with holy prayers: and 'tis spoken,
To the succeeding royalty he leaves
The healing benediction. With this strange virtue,
He hath a heavenly gift of prophecy,
And sundry blessings hang about his throne,
That speak him full of grace.

Enter Uncle Sam...

Joe Citizen

See, who comes here?

The Ghost of John Kennedy

My countryman; but yet I know him not.

Joe Citizen

My ever-gentle cousin, welcome hither.

The Ghost of John Kennedy

I know him now. Good God, betimes remove
The means that makes us strangers!

Uncle Sam

Sir, amen.

Joe Citizen

Stands the United States where it did?

Uncle Sam

Alas, poor country!
Almost afraid to know itself. It cannot
Be call'd our mother, but our grave; where nothing,
But who knows nothing, is once seen to smile;
Where sighs and groans and shrieks that rend the air
Are made, not mark'd; where violent sorrow seems
A modern ecstasy; the dead man's knell
Is there scarce ask'd for who; and good men's lives
Expire before the flowers in their caps,
Dying or ere they sicken.

Joe Citizen

O, Doctor
Too nice, and yet too true!

The Ghost of John Kennedy

What's the newest grief?

Uncle Sam

That of an hour's age doth hiss the speaker:
Each minute teems a new one.

Joe Citizen

How does my wife?

Uncle Sam

Why, well.

Joe Citizen

And all my children?

Uncle Sam

Well too.

Joe Citizen

The tyrant has not batter'd at their peace?

Uncle Sam

No; they were well at peace when I did leave 'em.

Joe Citizen

Speak up man: how goes't?

Uncle Sam

When I came hither to transport the tidings,
Which I have heavily borne, there ran a rumour
Of many worthy fellows that were out;
Which was to my belief witness'd the rather,
For that I saw the tyrant's power a-foot:
Now is the time of help; your eye on America
Would create soldiers, make our women fight,
To doff their dire distresses.

Act 4, Scene 3

The Ghost of John Kennedy

Be't their comfort
We are coming thither: gracious mass action hath
Lent us good Joe Citizen and ten thousand men;
An older and a better citizen soldier none
That the American Republic gives out.

Uncle Sam

Would I could answer
This comfort with the like! But I have words
That were transmitted by a secret code,
that which my intelligence sources tell me.

Joe Citizen

What concern they?
The general cause? Or is it a fee-grief
Due to some single breast?

Uncle Sam

No mind that's honest
But in it shares some woe; though the main part
Pertains to you alone.

Joe Citizen

If it be mine,
Keep it not from me, quickly let me have it.

Uncle Sam

Let not your ears despise my tongue for ever,
Which shall possess them with the heaviest sound
That ever yet they heard.

Joe Citizen

Hum! I guess at it.

Uncle Sam

Your castle is surprised; your wife and babes
Savagely slaughter'd by a practiced death squad;
To relate the manner, were, on the quarry of these
Murder'd deer, to add the death of you, they were tortured.

The Ghost of John Kennedy

Merciful heaven!
What, man! ne'er pull your hat upon your brows;
Give sorrow words: the grief that does not speak
Whispers the o'er-fraught heart and bids it break.

Joe Citizen

My children too?

Uncle Sam

Wife, children, servants, all
That could be found.

Joe Citizen

And I must be from thence!
My wife kill'd too?

Uncle Sam

I have said.

The Ghost of John Kennedy

Be comforted:
Let's make us medicines of our great revenge,
To cure this deadly grief.

Joe Citizen

All my pretty ones?
Did you say all? O hell! All?
What, all my pretty chickens and their hen
At one fell swoop? What, tortured and dismembered?

Act 4, Scene 3

The Ghost of Malcolm X

...come home to roost.

The Ghost of John Kennedy

Dispute it like a man.

Joe Citizen

I shall do so;
But I must also feel it as a man:
I cannot but remember such things were,
That were most precious to me. Did heaven look on,
And would not take their part? Sinful Joe Citizen!
They were all struck for thee!!! Naught that I am,
Not for their own demerits, but for mine own,
Fell slaughter on their souls. Heaven rest them now!

The Ghost of John Kennedy

Be this the whetstone of your sword: let grief
Convert to anger; blunt not the heart, enrage it.

Joe Citizen

O, I could play the woman with mine eyes
And braggart with my tongue! But, gentle heavens,
Cut short all intermission; front to front
Bring thou this fiend of treason and myself;
Within my sword's length set him; if he 'scape,
Heaven forgive him too!

The Ghost of John Kennedy

This tune goes manly.
Come, go we to the king; our power is ready;
Our lack is nothing but our leave; MacCain
Is ripe for shaking, and the powers above
Put on their instruments. Receive what cheer you may:
The night is long that never finds the day.

Exeunt

Act 5 Scene 1

MacCain's Luxury Penthouse Apartment.

Enter a CIA Doctor and a Cleaning Lady

CIA Doctor

I have two nights watched with you, but can perceive
No truth in your report. When was it she last walked?

Cleaning Lady

Since his majesty went into the field, I have seen
Her rise from her bed, throw her night-gown upon
Her, unlock her closet, take forth paper, fold it,
Write upon't, read it, afterwards seal it, and again
Return to bed; yet all this while in a most fast sleep.

CIA Doctor

A great perturbation in nature, to receive at once
The benefit of sleep, withal the ambian effects of
Watching! In this slumbery agitation, besides her
Walking and other actual performances, what, at any time,
Have you heard her say? To gainsay the recording.

Cleaning Lady

That, sir, which I will not report after her.

CIA Doctor

You may to me: and 'tis most meet you should.

Cleaning Lady

Neither to you nor any one; having no witness to
confirm my speech. A recording tape can be edited.

Act 5, Scene 1

Enter Lady MacCain, with a taper

Lo you, here she comes! This is her very guise;
And, upon my life, fast asleep. Observe her; stand close.

CIA Doctor

How came she by that light?

Cleaning Lady

Why, it stood by her: she has light by her continually; 'tis her command.

CIA Doctor

You see, her eyes are open.

Cleaning Lady

Ay, but their sense is shut.

CIA Doctor

What is it she does now? Look, how she rubs her hands.

Cleaning Lady

It is an accustomed action with her, to seem thus
Washing her hands: I have known her to continue in this
A quarter of an hour.

Lady MacCain

Yet here's a spot.

CIA Doctor

Hark! She speaks: I will set down what comes from her,
To satisfy my remembrance the more strongly.

Lady MacCain

Out, damned spot! Out, I say! —One: two: why,
Then, 'tis time to do't. —Hell is murky!— Fie, my
Lord, fie! A soldier, and afeard? What need we

fear who knows it, when none can call our power to account? — Yet who would have thought John Kennedy to have had so much blood in him.

CIA Doctor

Dis you hear that?

Lady MacCain

The thane of Fife had a wife: where is she now?— What, will these hands ne'er be clean?—No more o' That, my lord, no more o' that: You mar all with this starting.

CIA Doctor

Go to, go to; you have known what you should not.

Cleaning Lady

She has spoke what she should not, I am sure of that: Heaven knows what she has known.

Lady MacCain

Here's the smell of the blood still: All the perfumes of Arabia will not sweeten this little hand. Oh, oh, oh!

CIA Doctor

What a sigh is there! The heart is sorely charged.

Cleaning Lady

I would not have such a heart in my bosom for the Dignity of the whole body.

CIA Doctor

Well, well, well, —

Cleaning Lady

Pray God it be, sir.

CIA Doctor

This disease is beyond my practise: yet I have known

those which have walked in their sleep who have died
holily in their beds.

Lady MacCain

Wash your hands, put on your nightgown; look not so
pale.—I tell you yet again, Colby's buried; he
cannot come out on's grave.

CIA Doctor

Even so?

Lady MacCain

To bed, to bed! There's buzzing in the lobby:
come, come, come, come, give me your hand. What's
done cannot be undone.—To bed, to bed, to bed!

Exit Lady MacCain...

CIA Doctor

Will she go now to bed?

Cleaning Lady

Directly.

CIA Doctor

Foul whisperings are abroad: unnatural deeds
Do breed unnatural troubles: infected minds
To their deaf pillows will discharge their secrets:
More needs she the divine than the physician.
God, God forgive us all! Look after her;
Remove from her the means of all annoyance,
keeping 24 hour surveillance. So, good night:
I think, but dare not speak.

Cleaning Lady

Good night, good doctor.

Exeunt

Act 5 Scene 2
New York Outside the Safe House.

Drum and colours. Enter Ghost of MLK, Ghost of RFK, Ghost of FDR, Ghost of Lincoln, Ghost of McKinley, Ghost of Garfield and Security

Ghost of RFK

The public mass action is near, led on by The Ghost of JFK,
His uncle Joe Citizen and the good Uncle Sam:
Revenges burn in them; for their dear causes
Would to the bleeding and the grim alarm
Excite the mortified man.

Ghost of MLK

Near Central Park shall we well meet them;
That way are they coming.

Ghost of FDR

Who knows if a CNN crew will be with him?

Ghost of RFK

For certain, sir, it is not: I have a file
Of all the gentry: there is Joe Citizen's son,
And many unrough youths that even now
Protest their first of manhood.

Ghost of Lincoln

Act 5, Scene 2

What does the tyrant?

Ghost of McKinley

His Luxury Penthouse he strongly fortifies:
Some say he's mad; others that lesser hate him
Do call it valiant fury: but, for certain,
He cannot buckle his distemper'd cause
Within the belt of rule.

Ghost of Garfield

Now does he feel
His secret murders sticking on his hands;
Now minutely revolts upbraid his faith-breach;
Those he commands move only in command,
Nothing in love: now does he feel his title
Hang loose about him, like a giant's robe
Upon a dwarfish thief.

Ghost of FDR

Who then shall blame
His pester'd senses to recoil and start,
When all that is within him does condemn
Itself for being there?

Ghost of MLK

Well, march we on,
To give obedience where 'tis truly owed:
Meet we the medicine of the sickly commonwealth,
And with him pour we in our country's purge
Each drop of us.

Ghost of RFK

Or so much as it needs,
To dew the sovereign flower and drown the weeds.
Make we our march towards Central Park

   Exeunt, marching...

Act 5 Scene 3
Luxury Penthouse.

Enter MacCain, CIA Doctor, and Attendants...

MacCain

Bring me no more reports; let them fly all:
Till Central Park removes to my Penthouse apartment
I cannot taint with fear. What's the boy JFK Junior?
Why doesn't he go fly his little airplane, why doesn't he?
Was he not born of a dame? The spirits that know
All mortal consequences have pronounced me thus:
'Fear not, MacCain; no man that's born of a dame
Shall e'er have power upon thee.' Then fly,
false thanes, fly in your little airplanes
And mingle with the epicures: until like
Wellstone you stride aloft into a thunderstorm!

The mind I sway by and the heart I bear
Shall never sag with doubt nor shake with fear.

Enter a Servant...

The devil damn thee black, thou cream-faced loon!
Where got'st thou that goose look?

Servant

There is ten thousand—

MacCain

Act 5, Scene 3

Geese, you fool!

Servant

Soldiers, sir.

MacCain

Go prick thy face, and over-red thy fear,
Thou lily-liver'd boy. What soldiers, chump?
Death of thy soul! Those linen cheeks of thine
Are counsellors to fear. What soldiers, milk-face?

Servant

The American public, so please you.

MacCain

Take thy face hence.

Exit Servant...

Ollie! —I am sick at heart,
When I behold— Ollie, I say! —This push
Will cheer me ever, or disseat me now.
I have lived long enough: my way of life
Is fall'n into the sear, the yellow leaf;
And that which should accompany old age,
As honour, love, obedience, troops of friends,
I must not look to have; but, in their stead,
Curses, not loud but deep, mouth-honour, breath,
Which the poor heart would fain deny, and dare not. Oliver!

Enter Oliver North...

Oliver North

What is your gracious pleasure?

MacCain

What news more?

Oliver North

All is confirm'd, my lord, which was reported.

MacCain

I'll fight till from my bones my flesh be hack'd.
Give me my kevlar body armour.

Oliver North

'Tis not needed yet.

MacCain

I'll put it on.
Send out more patrols, skirr the barrios;
Arrest those that talk of fear. Give me mine armour.
How does your patient, doctor?

CIA Doctor

Not so sick, my lord,
As she is troubled with thick coming fancies,
That keep her from her rest.

MacCain

Cure her of that. With all your MKUltra,
Canst thou not minister to a mind diseased,
Pluck from the memory a rooted sorrow,
Raze out the written troubles of the brain
And with some sweet oblivious antidote
Cleanse the stuff'd bosom of that perilous stuff
Which weighs upon the heart?

CIA Doctor

Therein the patient
Must minister to himself.

MacCain

Throw medicine then to the dogs; I'll none of it.
Come, put mine armour on; give me my iPad!
Oliver, send out. Doctor, the thanes fly from me.
Come, sir, dispatch. If thou couldst, doctor, cast
The water of my land, find her disease,
And purge it to a sound and pristine health,
I would applaud thee to the very echo,
That should applaud again.—Pull't off, I say.—
What rhubarb, potion, or what purgative drug,
Would scour this rank mob hence? Hear'st thou of them?

CIA Doctor

Ay, my good lord; your royal preparation
Makes us hear something.

MacCain

Bring it on!
I will not be afraid of death and bane,
Till Central Park come up to my Penthouse.

CIA Doctor

[Aside] Were I far away, away and clear,
Profit again should hardly draw me here.

Exeunt

Act 5 Scene 4
By Central Park

Drum and colours. Enter The Ghost of JFK, Joe Citizen and Young Joe Citizen, Uncle Sam, The Ghost of MLK, The Ghost of RFK, The Ghost of FDR, The Ghost of Lincoln, The Ghost of McKinley, The Ghost of Garfield, The Ghost of McKinley, and Citizen Soldiers, marching.

The Ghost of JFK

Cousins, I hope the days are near at hand
That chambers will be safe.

The Ghost of RFK

We doubt it nothing.

The Ghost of MLK

What wood is this before us?

The Ghost of RFK

Central Park West

The Ghost of JFK

Pass out those stacks of Village Voice rags,
Let every citizen take up a sheet of newsprint
And bear't before him: thereby shall we shadow
The numbers of our host and make discovery
Err in report of us.

American People

It shall be done.

Act 5, Scene 4

Joe Citizen

We learn no other but the confident tyrant
Keeps still in his Penthouse, and will endure
Our setting down before 't.

The Ghost of JFK

'Tis his main hope:
For where there is advantage to be given,
Both more and less have given him the revolt,
And none serve with him but constrained things
Whose hearts are absent too.

Uncle Sam

Let our just censures
Attend the true event, and put we on
Such an industrious patriotic mass action.

Joe Citizen

The time approaches
That will with due decision make us know
What we shall say we have and what we owe.

Thoughts speculative their unsure hopes relate,
But certain issue strokes must arbitrate:
Towards which advance the civil contest.

   Exeunt, marching...

Act 5 Scene 5
MacCain's Penthouse Within

Enter MacCain, Oliver North, Felix Rodríguez, Thomas Clines,
Barry Seal, Frank Sturgis, Bernard Baker, E Howard Hunt, and
Special Forces Soldiers, with Heavy Metal Music pouring from
their Boom Boxes, all kinds of American Flag colours.

MacCain

Hang out our banners on the outward walls;
The cry is still *'They come:'* our castle's strength
Will laugh a siege to scorn: here let them lie
Till famine and the drain on funds eat them up:
Were they not forced with those that should be ours,
We might have met them dareful, beard to beard,
And beat them backward home.
A cry of women within
What is that noise?

Oliver North

It is the cry of women, my good lord.

Exit Oliver North

MacCain

I have almost forgot the taste of fears;
The time has been, my senses would have cool'd
To hear a night-shriek; and my blades of hair
Would at a dismal treatise rouse and stir
As life were in't: I have supp'd full with horrors;

Act 3, Scene 5

Direness, familiar to my slaughterous thoughts
Cannot once start me.

Re-enter Oliver North...

Wherefore was that cry?

North

The queen, my lord, is dead.

MacCain

She should have died hereafter;
There would have been a time for such a word.
To-morrow, and to-morrow, and to-morrow,
Creeps in this petty pace from day to day
To the last syllable of recorded time,
And all our yesterdays have lighted fools
The way to dusty death. Out, out, brief candle!
Life's but a walking shadow, a poor player
That struts and frets his hour upon the stage
And then is heard no more: it is a tale
Told by an idiot, full of sound and fury,
Signifying nothing.

Enter Abu Bakr Al-Baghdadi

Thou comest to use thy tongue; thy story quickly.

Abu Bakr Al-Baghdadi

Gracious my lord,
I should report that which I say I saw,
But know not how to do it.

MacCain

Well, say it them.

Abu Bakr Al-Baghdadi

As I did stand my watch upon the parapet,
I look'd toward Central, and anon, methought,
The wood began to move.

MacCain

Liar and terrorist rent-server!

Abu Bakr Al-Baghdadi

Let me endure your wrath, if't be not so:
Within this three mile may you see it coming;
I say, a moving grove, like a grove of birches, sir.

MacCain

If thou speak'st false,
in this fireplace you will be burned alive
Till you are roasted all over: if thy speech be sooth,
I pull in resolution, and begin
To doubt the equivocation of the fiend
That lies like truth: *'Fear not, till Central Park woods
Do come to my Luxury Penthouse'* and now a wood
Comes toward my apartments. Arm, arm, and out!

If this which he avouches does appear,
There is nor flying hence nor tarrying here.
I begin to be aweary of the sun,
And wish the estate o' the world were now undone.

Ring the alarum-bell! Blow, wind! come, wrack!
At least we will die with police gear on our back.

Exeunt

Act 5 Scene 6

On the Sidewalk Before MacCain's Penthouse.

Drum and colours. Enter Ghost of JFK, Joe Citizen, Uncle Sam, and demonstration of mass of public citizens with bright front pages of the Village Voice shining the summer sun. The Head-lines of the Papers scream "MacCain! Traitor!"

Ghost of JFK

Now near enough: your leafy screens throw down.
And show like those you are. You, worthy uncle,
Shall, with my cousin, your right-noble son,
Lead our first battle: worthy Uncle Sam and we
Shall take upon 's what else remains to do,
According to our order.

Joe Citizen

Fare you well.
Do we but find the tyrant's power to-night,
Let us be beaten, if we cannot fight now.

Uncle Sam

Make all our trumpets speak; give them all breath,
Those clamorous harbingers are of blood and death.

Exeunt

Act 5 Scene 7
Foyer of New York Luxury Apartment

Alarums. Enter MacCain

MacCain
They have tied me to a stake; I cannot fly,
But, bear-like, I must fight the course. What's he
That was not born of a dame? Such a one
Am I to fear, or none.

Enter Joe Citizen Junior...

MacCain
How did you get in here?

Joe Citizen Junior
Ha Ha Ha Your security is a joke.

MacCain
What? You punk!

Joe Citizen Junior
What is thy name?

MacCain
Thou'lt be afraid to hear it.

Joe Citizen Junior
No; though thou call'st thyself a hotter name
Than any is in hell.

Act 5, Scene 7

MacCain

My name's MacCain!

Joe Citizen Junior

The devil himself could not pronounce a title
More hateful to the ear of any American.

MacCain

No, nor more fearful.

Joe Citizen Junior

Thou liest, abhorred tyrant; with my sword
as with my pen, I'll prove the lie thou speak'st.
They fight and Joe Citizen Junior is shot in the same way
Oswald was bullet wound, where the victim is wincing as the
fatal shot goes into the gut.

MacCain

Thou was't born of a dame
Your swords I smile at, weapons laugh to scorn,
Brandish'd by man that's of a dame born.

Exit MacCain...
Alarums...
Enter The Ghost of JFK...

The Ghost of JFK

That way the noise is. Tyrant, show thy face!
If thou be'st slain and with no stroke of mine,
My wife and children's ghosts will haunt me still.
I cannot strike at wretched cut-out agents, whose arms
Are hired to bear their staves: either thou, MacCain,
Or else my sword with an unbatter'd edge
I sheathe again undeeded. There thou shouldst be;
By this great clatter, one of greatest note

Seems bruited. Let me find him, fortune!
And more I beg not.

Exit Ghost of JFK...
Alarums...
Enter Uncle Sam and Joe Citizen...

Joe Citizen

This way, my lord; the castle's gently render'd:
The tyrant's people on both sides do fight;
The noble thanes do bravely in the war;
The day almost itself professes yours,
And little is to do.

Uncle Sam

We have met with foes
That strike beside us.

Joe Citizen

Enter, sir, the Penthouse

Exeunt
Alarums...

Act 5 Scene 8
Luxury Pentouse Apartment
Overlooking Central Park

Enter MacCain

MacCain
Why should I play the Roman fool, and die
On mine own sword? whiles I see lives, the gashes
Do look better upon them.

Enter Uncle Sam...

Uncle Sam
Turn, hell-hound, turn!

MacCain
Of all men else I have avoided thee:
But get thee back; my soul is too much charged
With blood of thine already.

Uncle Sam
I have no words:
My voice is in my sword: thou bloodier villain
Than terms can give thee out!

They fight...

MacCain
You're wasting your time:

Act 5, Scene 8

As easy as you pass through air
your weapons are like nothing to me:
Go ahead, Pull the trigger. Take your shot!
I bear a charmed life, which must not yield,
To one of woman born.

Uncle Sam

Despair thy charm;
And let the angel whom thou still hast served
Tell thee, Uncle Sam is only a mythic character,
an embodiment of the faith of the American People.

MacCain

Accursed be that tongue that tells me so,
For it hath cow'd my better part of man!
And be these juggling fiends no more believed,
That palter with us in a double sense;
That keep the word of promise to our ear,
And break it to our hope. I'll not fight with thee.

Uncle Sam

Then yield thee, coward,
And live to be the show and gaze o' the time:
We'll have thee, as our rarer monsters are,
Painted on a pole, and underwrit,
'Here may you see the traitor'

MacCain

I will not yield,
To kiss the ground before the Ghost of JFK's feet,
And to be baited with the rabble's curse.
Though Central Park wood do come to my Penthouse,
And thou opposed, being of no dame born,
Yet I will try the last. Before my body
I throw my warlike shield. Lay on, Sam
And damn'd be him that first cries, *'Hold, enough!'*

Exeunt, fighting. Alarums Retreat. Flourish. Enter, with drum and colours, The Ghost of JFK, The Ghost of RFK, The Ghost of MLK, The Ghost of FDR, The Ghost of Lincoln, The Ghost of Garfield, The Ghost of McKinley, the other Thanes, and Soldiers

The Ghost of JFK

I would the friends we miss were safe arrived.

Joe Citizen

Some must go off: and yet, by these I see,
So great a day as this is cheaply bought.

Ghost of RFK

Your noble son.

Ghost of MLK

Your son, my lord, has paid a soldier's debt:
He only lived but till he was a man;
The which no sooner had his prowess confirm'd
In the unshrinking station where he fought,
But like a man he died.

Joe Citizen

Then he is dead?

Ghost of RFK

Ay, and brought off the field: your cause of sorrow
Must not be measured by his worth, for then
It hath no end.

Joe Citizen

Had he his orders?

Ghost of MLK

He rushed to the front.

Joe Citizen

Why then, God's soldier be he!
Had I as many sons as I have hairs,
I would not wish them to a fairer death:
And so, his knell is knoll'd.

The Ghost of JFK

He's worth more sorrow,
And that I'll spend for him.

Joe Citizen

He's worth no more
They say he parted well, and paid his score:
And so, God be with him! Here comes newer comfort.

Re-enter Uncle Sam, with MacCain's head

Uncle Sam

Hail, king! for so thou art: behold, where stands
The usurper's cursed head: the time is free:
I see thee compass'd with thy kingdom's pearl,
That speak my salutation in their minds;
Whose voices I desire aloud with mine:
Hail, the President of the United States!
That you are avenged brings honor to thee.

All

Hail, the honorable President of the United States!

Flourish...

The Ghost of JFK

We shall not spend a large expense of time
Before we reckon with your several loves,
You will want to be getting back to.
My thanes and kinsmen,
Henceforth be known as true patriots,
The first that ever New York such an honour named.
What's more to do,
Which would be planted newly with the time,
As calling home our exiled friends abroad
That fled the snares of watchful self-censorship
And political correctness.
Producing forth the cruel ministers
Of this dead butcher and his fiend-like queen,
Who, as 'tis thought, by self and violent hands
Took off her life; this, and what needful else
That calls upon us, by the grace of God
We will perform in measure, time and place:
So, thanks to all at once and to each one,
Whom we invite to a White House gala ball.

Flourish...
Exeunt

Vietnam, Laos and the "Phoenix Program"

In 1966, Theodore Shackley became the CIA station chief in Laos where he directed the CIA's secret war of pitting the Hmong people villagers against Vietnamese on the Ho Chi Minh Trail. In 1968, he moved on to become station chief for Vietnam and to head up Operation Phoenix, a secret assassination and forced disappearance program.

In 1971, the head of the CIA, William Colby, in testimony before Congress, admitted that the number of Vietnamese directly killed in this operation to be 20,000. Accurate mortality numbers, and the total number of victims, will never be known.

Operation Phoenix targeted the civilian population. Tortured bodies were strewn around villages of Vietnam. The so-called "Mexican Drug Gangs" do the same today: advertise their lurid crimes against humanity with a variety of monickers, similar to how the name-game is played by the obscene ISIS/ISIL/Al-Quaida terrorists.

One suspects that, in all of these cases, civilians are assassinated and "picked up" and "disappeared" in a body-count based system adopted by the USA military under the long-term influence of the CIA after the JFK hit, Thus, the systematic terrorization of national populations is the sad recurring hallmark of Operation Phoenix.

Cast of Characters

Victor Apodeca (May 31, 1937 — ?) A US airman shot down and taken prisoner in Vietnam. His sister testified at the US Senate MIA Committee where she was angrily rebuffed by Senator John MacCain, who famously huffed out of the session.

Abū Bakr al-Baghdadi (28 July 1971 —) Iman of Salafi jihadist militant terrorist organisation Islamic State of Iraq and the Levant (ISIL, ISIS, or whatever). Trained in Camp Bucca by his interrogators, released to lead Iraqi Sunni ex-Saddam Hussein's-army elements to wreak havoc in the region and to attack the government of Syrian President Hafaz al Asad. The infantry of Al-Baghdadi included criminals, drug addicts, mercenaries, and religious fanatics.

Bernard Leon Barker (March 17, 1917 – June 5, 2009) Barker joined the Cuban secret police under Fulgencio Batista. He reported to the Federal Bureau of Investigation (FBI) and worked for them as an undercover agent. He joined the 1961 Bay of Pigs invasion. was a Watergate burglar and undercover operative in CIA directed plots to overthrow Cuban leader Fidel Castro. Investigators have revealed evidence linking him to the assassination of President John F. Kennedy, including eyewitness accounts placing him at the grassy knoll in Dealey Plaza, Dallas, on November 22.

McGeorge "Mac" Bundy (March 30, 1919 – September 16, 1996) Like his father, he was inducted into the Skull and Bones secret society, nicknamed "Odin". He remained in contact with his fellow Bonesmen afterward. He graduated from Yale in the class of 1940. In 1941, he was awarded a three-year junior fellowship in Harvard Society of Fellows. He was selected for the Council on Foreign Relations in 1949. Became United States National Security Advisor to President John F. Kennedy from 1961. He was president of the Ford Foundation from 1966 through 1979. Chief architect of the escalation of USA aggression against Vietnam.

Tomas Clines (August 18, 1928 — July 30, 2013) Operation Phoenix operative. Faithful servant of the CIA. Cuba operations. Flush with state money and federal aid, the South Florida Task Force, harassed and arrested the Colombian cowboys criminal drug-running competition; Clines and his loyal co-workers took control of the Miami nexus.

William Colby (January 4, 1920 – April 27, 1996) Office of Strategic Services, then the newly created Central Intelligence Agency (CIA). Before and during the Vietnam War, Colby served as chief of station in Saigon, chief of the CIA's Far East Division, and head of the Civil Operations and Rural Development effort, as well as overseeing the Phoenix Program. After Vietnam, Colby became director of central intelligence.

Allen Dulles (April 7, 1893 – January 29, 1969) A troubled man with a morbid imagination. Dulles is reported to have been fascinated with watching a fly die on the point of a pin. As head of the Central Intelligence Agency (CIA), he oversaw the 1954 Guatemalan coup d'état and Operation Ajax (the overthrow of Iran's elected government). Following the Bay of Pigs debacle, Dulles and his entourage, including Deputy Director for Plans Richard M. Bissell Jr. and Deputy Director Charles Cabell, were forced to resign.

Donald Gregg (December 5, 1927 —) Operation Phoenix. CIA all the way. Chief honcho at El Salvador's covert operations at Ilopango Air Base. Bush man. All around bad boy. National Security Council advisor (1979–1982) and National Security Advisor to U.S. Vice President George H. W. Bush (1982–1989), United States Ambassador to Korea (1989–1993)

E. Howard Hunt (October 9, 1918 – January 23, 2007) CIA. Dirty tricks and Third World wet-works specialist. Writer of fiction. After President John F. Kennedy fired Dulles in 1961 for the Bay of Pigs disaster, Hunt "served" as the first Chief of Covert Action for the Domestic Operations Division (DODS) from 1962 to 1964. Hunt was arrested and convicted for organizing the bugging of the Democratic National Committee at the Watergate office building.

Curtis Lemay (November 15, 1906 – October 1, 1990) LeMay is discredited with designing and implementing an ineffective strategic bombing campaign in the Pacific theater of World War II. As Chief of Staff of the Air Force, he called for a sustained aerial bombing campaign against civilian infrastructure. Against all evidence, he spent his career justifying the effectiveness of air power against civilian targets.

Lyman Lemnitzer (August 29, 1899 – November 12, 1988) Chairman of the Joint Chiefs of Staff from 1960 to 1962 where he advocated massive aerial bombing of Vietnam. Advocated bombing Cuba. Supreme Allied Commander of NATO from 1963 to 1969. Avid proponent of the Strategic Bombing school of warfare. The movie, Doctor Strangelove: this is Lemnitzer.

Edward Lansdale (February 6, 1908 – February 23, 1987) United States Air Force officer in the Office of Strategic Services and the Central Intelligence Agency (CIA). Old Asia hand. Operation Phoenix. An early proponent of aggressive covert U.S. actions in the Third World

David Morales (August 26, 1925 - May 8, 1978) CIA operative in Cuba and Chile. Executive Action, a series of projects designed to kill foreign leaders deemed unfriendly to the United States. Operation PBSUCCESS, the CIA covert operation that overthrew the democratically elected President of Guatemala, Jacobo Arbenz Guzmán. JMWAVE, the ZRRIFLE plot to assassinate Fidel Castro, the Bay of Pigs Invasion operation, the CIA's secret war in Laos, the extrajudicial execution of Che Guevara, and the overthrow of Salvador Allende and take-over of the Chilean economy.

Oliver North (October 7, 1943 —) National Security Council staff member during the Iran–Contra affair, involved in the illegal sale of weapons to Iran. North used the proceeds from the arms-deal with Iran to supply counter-revolutionary mercenaries on the Miskito Coast of Nicaragua and mercenary military training bases in Honduras and El Salvador. However, support for the Contra rebel groups in Nicaragua had been specifically prohibited under the Boland Amendment; thus the scandal.

Robert Strange MacNamara (June 9, 1916 – July 6, 2009) Secretary of Defense, from 1961 under President John F. Kennedy. Played a major role in escalating the United States war against Vietnam. Responsible for the institution of systems analysis in public policy (sometimes referred to as: b.s.) which developed into the discipline known today as: policy analysis (otherwise called: boondoggle). Believed that all information could be quantified and used to make decisions. He applied this theory to bombing strategies during the Second World War as a member of the United States Army Air Force and dead body-count methodology in Vietnam.

Félix Rodríguez (31 May 1941 —) Cuban American. Central Intelligence Agency Paramilitary Operations Officer. Big man in the Bay of Pigs Invasion and in the hunting-down and the execution of Che Guevara in the backcountry of Bolivia. Rodriguez's El Salvador Ilopango Air Base gun-and-drug-running operation was exposed in the Iran-Contra scandal.

Walt Whitman Rostow (October 7, 1916 — February 13, 2003) American political theorist, prominent for his role in the shaping of US foreign policy in Southeast Asia during the 1960s. Advisor to President Kennedy. Tireless tout of the "free enterprise system". Consistent advocate of aggression against the Vietnamese population. Rostow warned that "The Communists" were destroying freedom and the American way of life, and that the communists were enemies of democracy in the Third World. Rostow promoted big military responses by the USA, even to political challenges in far-away jungles.

Barry Seal (July 16, 1939 — February 19, 1986) Operation Phoenix. CIA. Adler Berriman "Barry" Seal CIA pilot who disguised himself as a notorious drug smuggler.

Theodore Shackley (July 16, 1927 — December 9, 2002) CIA station chief in Laos between 1966–1968. Saigon station chief from 1968 through February 1972. Director of the "Phoenix Program" a special project initiated in Vietnam wherein civilians were identified by U.S. intelligence officers to be targeted for forced disappearance, harsh interrogation, and anonymous death. The program included torture to terrorize the population. In Vietnam, Operation Phoenix soon turned into an enormous extortion racket, as people paid to not be on the list. In 1976, Shackley was appointed Associate Deputy Director for Operations, in charge of CIA covert operations.

www.ingramcontent.com/pod-product-compliance
Lightning Source LLC
Chambersburg PA
CBHW051829040426
42447CB00006B/445